What readers and the media say about Atlanta attorney John C. Mayoue and his previous book, *Southern Divorce:*

"In his book, ... (Mayoue) ... addresses the why of Southern divorce, although the book primarily functions as a guide for people seeking or considering a divorce. It explains the legal process and issues, as well as the emotional and logistical elements — specifically successful divorce."

Arkansas Democrat Gazette

"The Ted Turner-Jane Fonda split after 10 years together shows how a big divorce can be made almost to disappear if handled well."

W Magazine

"Mayoue is a 'go-to' guy in high profile divorces."

Atlanta Journal Constitution

"John Mayoue makes... (divorce)...more bearable with his insight in dealing with the process."

Marianne Rogers, ex-wife of singer Kenny Rogers

"High-powered Atlanta attorney John C. Mayoue's guide for the unhappily hitched. Don't get mad, get maintenance, custody and equitable division of assets."

Atlanta Magazine

"This book (Southern Divorce) is a little bit of Southern culture, and a lot of help for divorcing people."

Lynne Russell, former CNN anchor

PROTECTING YOUR ASSETS FROM A GEORGIA DIVORCE

John C. Mayoue
Attorney at Law

Published by PSG Books
Dallas, Texas

Protecting Your Assets
From A Georgia Divorce

John C. Mayoue
PSG Books
9603 White Rock Trail, Suite 312   Dallas, Texas 75238
214/340-6223   214/340-6209 fax
upshaw@psgbooks.com

Books published under the PSG Books imprint are available in bookstores and at Amazon.com, BN.com, PSGBooks.com and other online retailers. Resellers and affinity groups wishing to purchase books in quantity at a discount may contact PSG Books toll free at (800) 465-1508.

Contact John C. Mayoue to speak to groups on the financial aspects of divorce. He can be reached at the law firm of Warner, Mayoue, Bates & Nolen, P.C., 3350 Riverwood Parkway, Suite 2300, Atlanta, Georgia 30339, (770) 951-2700 voice, (770) 951-2200 facsimile, jmayoue@wmbnlaw.com.

ISBN 978-0-9659273-6-9
Manufactured in the United States of America

9 8 7 6 5 4 3 2 1

Library of Congress Cataloging-in-Publication Data

Mayoue, John C., 1954-
    Protecting your assets from a Georgia divorce / John C.
Mayoue.
        p. cm.
    Summary: "Provides detailed information on divorce, child
custody, complex property settlements and other financial aspects of dissolving a marriage specifically in the state of Georgia, complete with checklists, advice on surviving the process
and guidelines to help you emerge financially and emotionally
intact"--Provided by publisher.
    ISBN 978-0-9659273-6-9
    1. Divorce settlements--Georgia--Popular works. 2. Equi-
table distribution of marital property--Georgia--Popular works.
I. Title.
    KFG100.Z9M39 2007
    346.75801'664--dc22

                                        2007005440

NOTICE AND DISCLAIMER

State laws, legal precedents, tax codes and regulations vary greatly from one jurisdiction to another and change over time. The reader should not use this book for specific legal advice. Every divorce case and post-divorce action is unique, requiring the advice of those versed in the laws of the jurisdiction where the action is taken. It must be understood, therefore, that this book will provide readers with a general overview of financial matters related to the divorce process and post-divorce issues, so they may take legal action or otherwise address these issues better informed.

Reading this book does not establish an attorney-client relationship between the reader and the authors. Consult an attorney for specific information related to your personal situation.

TABLE OF CONTENTS

Part One

Considering Action

Chapter 1

Divorce Can Cause Financial Hardship • Divorce: By the Numbers • A Georgia Divorce's Financial Reality • Consider Reconciliation • Sticking It Out for The Kids? • Planning Your Divorce Strategy

SNAPSHOT:
One Marriage. Two Perspectives.

Chapter 2

Can You Remain Friends With Your Spouse? • Time to Gather Information • Seven Simple Steps to Prepare for Divorce • Think Strategically

Chapter 3

Representing Yourself • Benefits of a Specialist • Initial Interviews • Questions to Ask Your Attorney • Yes to Experience, No to Guarantees

Chapter 4

The New Realities: Mediation and Collaborative Law • Attorneys Must Withdraw If Settlement Fails • Locate a Collaborative Lawyer

SNAPSHOT:
A More Humane Method

SNAPSHOT:
To Her a Drunk, To Him a Loving Dad

Part Two

Dividing Assets and Debts

SNAPSHOT:
It's Her Separate Property

12 Steps to a More Productive Divorce

SNAPSHOT:
Who Can Afford the Family Home?

SNAPSHOT:
Dental Practice A Major Asset

Who Gets the Business? • Valuing the Business • Favored Business Entities • Tax Liabilities of the Business

SNAPSHOT:
The Sometimes Forgotten Assets

SNAPSHOT:
The Ultimate Loss of Identity

Part Three
Look to the Future

SNAPSHOT:
No Clear Link between Child Support and Visitation

Health Insurance for the Children • Health Insurance for Your Spouse
• Life Insurance Protects Future Payments

SNAPSHOT:
Helping Her Regain Her Balance

Absurd Statements Your Divorce Lawyer Should Correct

SNAPSHOT:
Relocation, A National Hot-Button Issue

INTRODUCTION/ACKNOWLEDGEMENTS

Divorce, no matter how civilized or cooperative, is never good or positive. What increased to monumental proportions in the 1960s and 70s as a major experiment in personal freedom is rightly blamed for many of society's ills. The idea of a family dissolving is a tragedy in the making, and we should mourn its loss.

In the state of Georgia alone, more than 30,000 divorces are finalized each year. That's a lot of dislocation for the divorcing parties, their children, extended families and friends.

Those of us who make our living dealing with divorce know this dislocation gives rise to all kinds of misinformation. This book is about correcting incorrect assumptions, dispelling myths and rumors and generally providing the latest information about a Georgia divorce to those going through the process. We don't need to use this book to increase business. As you see, there are already too many divorces in this state, and there's plenty of business to go around. The Atlanta law firm that I practice in is one of the largest in the country that handles only divorce. One of my colleagues once said that in a perfect world, there would be no divorce and we would practice another kind of law entirely.

But since divorce is apparently here to stay, we do a better job for our clients when they become educated about the laws and customs surrounding divorce. In every case, this is better than relying on what Aunt Minnie said her daughter received in spousal support, child support and the couple's property division when she divorced 10 years ago in Georgia, or was that in Alabama? Changes in the law over time and in different jurisdictions make a reference work like this essential to people who are about to turn their lives over to a system that can be harsh and unforgiving.

Divorce is difficult, no doubt about it, and those who face this process with little understanding can harm their lives and the lives of their children for decades to come. I crafted this work with the idea that instead of paying a lawyer's hourly rate for the first few consultations, you can get the same information just by reading this one book.

In my first book for a general audience, *Southern Divorce* (PSG Books 2004), I detailed the high rate of divorce in the southern states, including Georgia, and talked about the panic that set in among state officials, the clergy and the public at large as they saw divorce threatening the very existence of families in the 1980s and 90s. All across the south, efforts to reduce the incidence of divorce have included requiring a couple to seek counseling before getting married, moving to legalize covenant marriage and extending the waiting period before a divorce can be final.

In Georgia, it seems the most effective method of curbing divorce statistics has been to quit reporting them on a statewide basis. At one time, it was the job of Superior Court clerks across the state to collect divorce statistics and report them to the State Registrar of Vital Records, who would pass them along to the U.S. Census Bureau for use in various reports. Now the state has discontinued its count. To find out the number of Georgia divorces, you would have to call each Superior Court clerk in the state. Without a total, I suppose you can't prove that we have a crisis.

Divorce will always be with us, no matter what laws we pass or how wrong we feel it is. So there will always be a place for effective settlement techniques, divorce recovery classes and books like this one. If any of these help just one family to heal the wounds that divorce can inflict and begin to move forward in life, they are worth the time and effort.

I want to thank the many people who helped to make this book a reality. I especially appreciate those people who have so graciously allowed me to represent them through the years. Your experiences form the knowledge base that I called upon to bring life to the various scenarios and situations that the reader can expect to confront during a divorce or post-divorce matter.

Family law has become so complex that no single person can master every aspect of the most difficult cases. I want to thank the many experts in divorce-related activities—accountants, financial planners, family therapists, mortgage brokers, appraisers, real estate brokers, certified divorce planners, and attorneys in other specialties—for contributing their expertise to this effort. In Appendix A, we list many of Georgia's most qualified experts in these various professional fields as they apply to divorce.

Lastly, I want to thank Noble Sprayberry, my editor at PSG Books, for his attention to this work. Over several months of the editing process, he helped to shape my thoughts into the book you are holding today.

John C. Mayoue

About the Author

John C. Mayoue is one of the best-known divorce attorneys in Georgia. His clients have included Marianne Gingrich, ex-wife of former U.S. House Speaker Newt Gingrich; actress Jane Fonda, communications mogul Ted Turner's ex; and former big league baseball star David Justice, ex-husband of actress Halle Berry; Janice Holyfield, former wife of heavyweight boxing champion Evander Holyfield; and Marianne Rogers, ex-wife of country singer Kenny Rogers.

One of his most famous cases was that of "Baby Gregory," whose parents were accused of abuse by Tennessee officials. The baby's mother abducted the baby and took him to a children's hospital in Atlanta. Later, Mayoue and one of his law partners won a ruling that the parents were not negligent and that Baby Gregory belonged with them.

Mayoue attended Transylvania University in Kentucky and Emory School of Law and settled in Atlanta after graduation.

He decided to specialize in divorce litigation because of the profound effect it has on people. "Here you're dealing with something that's real," he says. "There's emotion attached to it. Real, live people need help and you can give it."

Mayoue is a prolific writer on divorce for other lawyers and the general public. His books include *Georgia Jurisprudence, Family Law* (West Group 2006); *Southern Divorce* (PSG Books 2004); *Balancing Competing Interests in Family Law* (American Bar Association 2003); and *How to Plan and Conduct Family Law Discovery* (ICLE 1994). In addition, he was a contributing author to *The Morality of Adoption* (Wm. B. Eerdmans 2005) and *The Joy of Settlement* (American Bar Association 1997). He often speaks to civic and parent groups on the various facets of family law.

Part One

Considering Action

1

Hope for the Best,
Prepare for the Worst

Georgia represents the New South's heart, a bustling economic engine reshaping the culture of neighborhoods, cities and rural communities. Few touchstones show a greater change than marriage and a fundamental shift from traditional Bible Belt beliefs appearing in the form of divorce. An explosion of failed marriages hit this state in the 1960s and 70s. While signs indicate a leveling off of divorce rates, the cultural shock wave continues to reverberate through the courts today.

The texture of divorce isn't consistent in a state often defined by our idea of two Georgias: The Atlanta metropolitan area creates a unique whole. Everything else falls to the rest of the state.

People living amid big city bustle often adopt starkly different views of marriage from those living in the state's smaller communities. Divorce exists in both worlds, but the reasons and emotional weight frequently differ. "What you end up with is far more contested divorces in the country than in the city," says John Witte, director of the Center for the Study of Law and Religion at Emory University in Atlanta. "There's far heavier use of jury trials as opposed to bench trials and a far longer divorce process in the country than in the city."

The difference is less urban versus rural than it is small, intensely connected communities versus a more anonymous city life. A deep stigma against divorce and hope of avoiding an abundance of small-town curiosity holds many fragmenting marriages together. When those bonds break, anger and an effort to cast blame often defines the divorce. "In the city, divorce is often just another transaction gone bust and it needs to be worked through with maximum respect for all parties concerned. With the stakes being high, there's a good battle to grab what you can," Witte says.

Georgia courts are increasingly adopting tools to keep marriages together as the state moves away from the easy-out process of the early '80s and '90s.

Shifts include additional counseling requirements and biases away from litigation and in favor of mediation and other forms of alternative dispute resolution. There is a trend to find better options than a one-time marital property division, particularly when a divorce involves children. Courts are also somewhat more responsive to considering fault in the assessment of property division, even though Georgia is a no-fault state and fault isn't the basis for the divorce itself.

Few doubt the financial stakes. "We know that for every three divorces, one family ends up below the poverty line," says Dr. Steven Nock, a family demographer and professor of sociology at the University of Virginia. "The average woman with dependent children who ends up in poverty stays poor for about eight months. The federal government pays for part of that, but states pay the balance. Divorce is a major economic issue."

DIVORCE: BY THE NUMBERS

Total divorces granted in the U.S. each year:
1.1 million

State with the lowest divorce rate:
Massachusetts

State with the highest divorce rate:
Nevada

Estimated average length of divorce from start to finish:
1 year

Number of divorced people nationwide:
19.4 million

Number of divorced people in Georgia during Census 2000:
656,777

Estimated median age at first marriage in Georgia: Men,
26.3 years old (national median, 26.7); Women, 24.4 years old
(national median, 25.1).

Estimated number of American children involved in divorce:
1.075 million

Percent of all children living with a divorced parent:
40

Average cost of a wedding:
$22,000

Average cost of a divorce:
$36,000

DIVORCE CAN CAUSE FINANCIAL HARDSHIP

Divorce rates peaked nationally between the 1960s and the early 1980s, with southern states such as Georgia leading the trend. Many people coming of age in that 20-year span learned the financial uncertainty of divorce. Those who married multiple times faced a repeated monetary ebb and flow, increasing their net worth during marriage and reducing it after each divorce. The financial toll of divorce can extend from the individual to his or her children and extended families. It's often a painful cycle. Emotional crisis increases financial woes, which in turn creates even more emotional upheaval. Faced with high stakes, anyone considering a divorce should go through a systematic reality check.

People often decide on divorce before facing the financial realities, or even calculating their net worth. A true accounting often arrives only when it's time to divide assets. The bottom line often brings a shock, a first-time tally of a marriage's accumulated wealth. The worth of a seemingly middle-class family may reach several million dollars when considering home equity, personal property, retirement funds and possibly the value of a business.

But the reverse can hold true. Some unions create more debt than assets, leaving a thin financial foundation. Consider a family living in a large home, driving new cars, sending their kids to private schools and vacationing several times annually. Such a driven lifestyle capped by divorce can leave some couples with large debts and few assets.

And never assume one spouse will come out ahead in divorce, which can often force a shared burden for both the payor spouse and recipient spouse. The payor spouse is the one who might keep a business or other assets that cannot be divided but who may have to make payments to a recipient spouse to compensate for receiving the lion's share of the estate. These payments can devastate the finances of a payor spouse, but also leave the recipient spouse struggling. The total payment rarely equals the amount of money that person spent monthly before divorce.

Money that maintained one household must now support two, despite the expectations of the parties to the divorce. No court order can stretch money far enough to guarantee the same lifestyle enjoyed before divorce for two people now living separate lives.

Imagine doubling every monthly household expense and attempting to pay these bills with the same monthly income. Few families could bear that burden without running a serious deficit or drastically curtailing their lifestyle. Both spouses feel entitled to the savings account, retirement funds and the equity in the family home. And most claim the other created the debts.

Raw emotions, serious financial stakes and an uncomfortable, if not outright contentious process can create a range of reactions in divorcing couples. Allowing anger or the need for a quick resolution to guide decisions often leads to poor outcomes.

During the heat of divorce, fiscally astute people often prove their own worst enemy, becoming entangled in the emotional and financial aspects of divorce. Anxious for a quick resolution, one person may agree to a poorly conceived settlement just to bring closure. A swift end to a marriage, though, often leaves one spouse with a financially unstable future.

Others might react far differently, allowing the need for revenge to cloud their judgment. For them, giving all of the money to a lawyer and other professionals sounds better than letting a "no-good ex" keep even pocket change once a divorce concludes.

Still others hope a court can work out a divorce in a financially fair way. A court, though, can only divide assets according to the law and the evidence, and that's not always equitable to both parties.

"A fair divorce is sort of like a friendly divorce. It's an oxymoron," says Lawrence C. Adams, director of the private Pastoral Counseling Service in Atlanta. "It sometimes happens, but in a very small percentage of the time. I don't think the law has ever talked about being fair. The law is just, and what's just is what can be negotiated and accepted. But fair doesn't really play into those divorces."

Surviving the financial impact of divorce requires both parties to determine their needs and the options each person has for meeting those needs. Anyone still deciding whether to divorce or who believes a spouse might soon file should adopt one priority: plan now.

Both parties to a divorce should determine their needs and the options each has for meeting those needs. Examine the household budget. Study income sources, expenses, assets and liabilities. Learn the most advantageous division of assets and debts in the divorce.

THE FINANCIAL REALITIES OF A GEORGIA DIVORCE

Reality #1: Divorces can be final in as few as 30 days, although very complex divorces and those that go to trial may not be final for months or even years.

Reality #2: Once a divorce is filed and one party wants to go through with it, you can't stop it from happening. Unless you and your spouse reconcile, your assets will be divided and you will be divorced.

Reality #3: Contentious, litigated divorces are more financially devastating than agreed upon settlements.

Reality #4: Your property may be divided in a way that is not equal. The judge or a jury may look at future earning capacity, fault for the divorce and other criteria when making a disproportionate division.

Reality #5: If one spouse proves that an asset is his or her separate property, the judge must award that asset to that person, although it might later be awarded to the other spouse as alimony.

Reality #6: Unless you have no significant assets or means to support yourself and you have been married for a significant time, or you and your spouse agree to it, in most cases there will be no alimony once the divorce is final.

Reality #7: The spouse who does not have primary custody of the children will, in practically every case, pay child support.

Reality #8: If the other side requests your financial information, you have to comply unless you settle. Even then, the other side may not agree without getting a look at your complete financial picture.

Reality #9: Your spouse can still file for bankruptcy after the divorce, leaving you with the responsibility for certain debts he or she was ordered to pay.

Reality #10: It is difficult to reopen a case or prevail on appeal, so get everything you possibly can from the property settlement the first time around.

CONSIDER RECONCILIATION

When weighing all your options, gauge the possibility of successfully keeping a marriage intact. Staying married usually presents the most productive alternative financially, while also allowing your family to remain whole. If there's a way to end differences, you owe it to yourself and your children to explore the possibilities.

Far more than any other reason, the breakup of many marriages stems from arguments over money. After World War II, a time of unbridled prosperity in this country, divorce increased dramatically. Does more money simply buy more time to quarrel over money?

Once men earned all the household income and held the power to decide how to spend it. Women, meanwhile, stayed home and cared for the children. Today's prevalence for two-income households means families must reach a consensus on an endless series of purchases.

Intense disagreements can fester, growing from one-time discussions to long-running and sweeping arguments over spending. Final decisions can leave raw, slow-to-heal wounds. Should we invest more into the retirement plan or take the beach vacation? Did a painfully expensive ticket for speeding in a school zone reduce the amount of the money we put aside for property taxes? How on earth can we possibly afford private school and soccer for the kids at the same time?

Many of these questions involve major decisions of lifestyle and purpose, affecting the future of you and your children. Individual traits such as selfishness or insecurity often bubble to the surface, adding deeply personal elements to the mix. It's a lot less expensive to consider if a therapist or psychiatrist may help to solve these problems.

"I think it's often very, very useful," Lawrence Adams says of therapy. "Some people have efficient and useful support systems and other people around who can enable them to move through a divorce. But I do think therapy is one useful tool. Friends are a useful tool. Healthy spiritual resources are an important component."

Also consider professionals. A credit counselor or financial planner can look at the overall picture and allocate resources, solving some problems. An experienced financial planner will offer instructions on how to pay taxes and bills before splurging on luxuries, while still allowing an occasional reward. It may take a professional to make one spouse or the other understand some hard financial realities. Just because you went to an exclusive private school doesn't mean your children can attend the same school if you don't have the money.

Many churches offer counseling for those in dire financial straits, often providing services at reduced rates, even free, for those with nowhere else to turn. Getting help when needed is critical, because a few painless financial compromises can save thousands of dollars and years of grief.

STICKING IT OUT FOR THE KIDS?

In the 1950s, when divorce was rare, the conventional wisdom held that people should stay together for the children. Three decades of high divorce rates forced the realization that divorce is no short-term fix for marital problems. Divorce creates an emotional drain and may bring more financial woes than the marriage itself.

Authors such as therapist Judith Wallerstein paint a dim picture for children of divorce. Her 25-year landmark study of 131 children of divorce centered on the painful search of these lost children, now adults, who struggled to overcome the feeling that love and trust are doomed.

Other authors offer a more up-beat perspective. Sociologist E. Mavis Hetherington wrote *For Better or For Worse: Divorce Reconsidered*. Hetherington tracked nearly 1,400 families and more than 2,500 children. Seventy-five to 80% of the children of divorce in her study indicated very little long-term damage from their parents' divorce. The other 20 to 25% of children from divorced families suffered varying emotional or psychological problems compared to 10% of children from intact families.

Staking out the debate's middle ground, sociologist Constance Ahrons wrote *We're Still Family: What Grown Children Have to Say About Their Parents' Divorce*. In a study of 173 grown children, almost 80% felt their parents were better off today and didn't wish their parents had remained together. These grown children felt better off or not affected by a long-ago divorce, while 20% had "life-long scars that didn't heal."

Most therapists and marriage counselors today believe you should only stay together for the children if you can maintain a reasonably healthy relationship. Talk to divorced parents to determine the pros and cons of their situations. Good information can help you make the right decision. Exhaust every resource, every option for keeping a marriage together.

Life-changing decisions, such as whether to stay married or divorce, require patience. Make the choice when feeling calm and centered, after you have taken as much time as you need to explore all options.

Critical exceptions, however, do exist. Relationships involving abusive, violent or other unacceptable behavior may leave no time to seek legal advice. Make an immediate decision for the welfare of your children. Then, get sound legal advice and use the justice system to prevent further deterioration of the situation.

A relationship doesn't have to be abusive to create financial and emotional damage. In the 1970s and early 1980s, the percentage of first-time marriages resulting in divorce peaked at about 65%. Fortunately, those percentages have fallen over the past decade. The reasons for the decrease are twofold: fewer people marry (as a percentage of the population), and those who marry wait until later in life. Greater maturity means they can often better shoulder the responsibility of marriage. That maturity seems to have reduced the number of marriages that end on a whim.

In our experience, people now look at divorce more realistically. They seem more capable of assessing the downside of divorce. Some high schools in Georgia even offer classes on marriage, focusing on responsibility and the importance of the institution. When people choose divorce, the decision should come from an informed position and not because of a silly spat.

Nationally about 43% of first marriages end in divorce. That's a lot of anger and confusion, both emotionally and financially. When people feel that way, few things are more cathartic than making a decision.

It's a scary but often liberating moment for many people. You accept an immediate future of tight household budgets. You understand new challenges of taking care of your family. And you understand there's no fun in sifting through the financial details of your life with this person. By making the decision to divorce, though, you can shape your future.

Planning Your Divorce Strategy

Many marriages begin with painstaking care, with fussing over how many ushers and bridesmaids to outfit, the frosting on the groom's cake and what type of music will make the reception. A professional wedding planner effectively coordinates the myriad details. Wouldn't it be prudent to hire an equally well-versed expert if a marriage dissolves?

Divorce planners are usually financial planners or analysts with experience helping people cope with the vagaries of divorce and its financial aftermath. In Georgia, they can earn the designation of Certified Divorce Financial Analyst. These experts don't plan for divorce as much as they help analyze the financial aspects of divorce.

They guide you in gathering critical financial paperwork such as account statements, which often disappear once a divorce begins. They help identify assets such as business interests and even frequent flyer miles. They offer guidance in developing a post-divorce budget before negotiations, helping to ensure a manageable settlement.

There is a difference, though, between planning and taking calculated steps to hide or dispose of assets. Planning is good. If you move into divorce with little forethought, you may set yourself up for lifelong disaster. Considering the dire consequences of inaction, assertive action will help you achieve a successful financial divorce.

Don't confuse this kind of planning with hiding assets. Never hide assets from your estranged partner or the court. Anyone who tries is usually caught, and the legal consequences can prove dire.

S N A P S H O T

ONE MARRIAGE. TWO PERSPECTIVES.

His View

He saw her as dynamic, a whirlwind of ambition who wanted to contribute to society and build on her budding marketing career with a Fortune 500 company. They made the perfect fit, everyone agreed. He would slowly take over his father's textile company. They wanted children, eventually. And, they could have everything they desired.

Somewhere in seven years of marriage, though, something went awry and he couldn't tell you how it happened. She came from a family of modest means and worried incessantly about the future.

He enjoyed the fruits of his labor: season tickets to college football, a couple rounds of golf each week with clients, and a comfortable SUV. They both worked hard, no doubt. She made vice president, and he took over from his father years earlier than expected.

But it was never enough for her. She needled him in front of his friends and family about how they needed to watch every penny to pay for all of his "toys." She resisted but he eventually convinced her to tap their savings to invest in a startup company owned by one of his college buddies, and he took more when the business needed another financial push.

She put on weight, and the idea of children took on greater urgency. A day didn't pass that she didn't fret out loud about how much she wanted children. To him, it wasn't a priority.

To satisfy her they hired a maid. A service did the laundry. She never cooked. He didn't want a 1950s wife, but occasionally a home-cooked dinner instead of eating out wasn't much to ask.

She spent more and more time away from him, with her own family. Her sister even revealed that his wife had a sexual affair with a handsome friend from college. He challenged her but she denied everything and said he wouldn't need to worry if he'd make it home more often. But she worked just as much as he did, often not ending her commute until late at night.

Once he understood this pitched battle was not going to subside, he began to consider the possibility that they might not live their entire lives together. He came into the marriage with several million dollars of non-liquid assets, including stocks, bonds and the family business. Property owned before the marriage normally is not subject to division by the court, although the court may divide increases in the value of these properties. The only property they owned together was a lovely home they bought the year they married.

When he needed money, he simply refinanced the house, which rose in value because of its suburban Atlanta location. He preserved his separate property while they spent most of their marital assets.

As he came to realize divorce was certain, he stopped even discussing money with her. He hoped she'd get the idea their money was separate, and his father's hard-earned business was his.

Her View

She, meanwhile, knew that she'd married a spendthrift, liar and thief. From the moment they married, he was on her case. He complained that she was overweight, although he always wanted to eat lavish meals in restaurants. Besides, he gained weight himself. And he never wanted to discuss beginning a family.

Everything was different before the marriage. He seemed a caring, committed person willing to let her enjoy her own career. He told her he would support her decisions as long as she was with him. She was his princess, his partner and never once before they married did he talk about her lack of skills as a housewife.

How could she possibly have a career and do all of the things he wanted. There wasn't enough time in the day. She commuted 90 minutes each way, largely because he wanted to live outside the city, and he only drove half that time to his office. She was good at her job and new projects rained down.

He was really married to the golf course and he expected her to be a dutiful golfing wife. She tried hard to like that lifestyle, but she didn't. Waiting around while others played bored her, and so did his friends. And when he criticized her, she went further into her shell.

She felt so out of place with his buddies that she spent time with her own friends and family. He resented that and his resentment played havoc with her self-esteem. She enjoyed the compliments of an old friend. But her sister was jealous of her and told her husband that she and the man were having an affair. Nothing was further from the truth.

Then, she noticed a big difference. He stopped criticizing her and just fell silent. He began to talk about divorce, but she just shrugged him off. If she could get him to forget about divorce, maybe things could be like they were at the start. He began to conserve his money. He spent more time at the office, even taking more business trips. She didn't know what was worse – his criticism or him ignoring her.

She was sure he was hiding money somewhere, perhaps in an offshore account. They refinanced the house and then the money was gone. And the startup owned by his buddy went bust, taking nearly all of their savings with it. He didn't seem upset by this and shrugged that they would soon make up the loss.

She knew they'd reached an end and she didn't care anymore. She had her own career and, luckily, they didn't have children to get caught in the middle.

The Result

The divorce started seven years into the marriage. Because they had no children, the division of property was the major issue. He had been very careful, since early in the marriage, to keep his property separate, and he didn't commingle any income from that property.

She thought there would be plenty of money to divide. He knew they had spent most of their marital assets. Then, they started throwing accusations at each other. She accused him of cruelty. He shot back that she was an adulteress. She was certain he was hiding assets from her and she ran up legal bills looking for hidden money, but found none. She hovered near depression and just wanted the marriage to end.

The steady appreciation in the value of their home provided the only divisible asset. He decided to give her all the furnishings in the home, as well as all of the remaining savings they'd accrued, as an inducement to ratify the property settlement during sessions with a mediator. She walked away with those furnishings, her personal belongings and investments worth approximately $150,000 in cash. After paying $97,000 in attorney fees, she walked away with $53,000. She earned $91,000 annually, enough to thrive on her own.

But after seven years of marriage, she was devastated. She was starting over.

2

Define the Type of Divorce You'll Have

Decisions don't end with the choice to divorce. You should follow that step with a consideration for the type of divorce you want. What relationship do you desire with your soon-to-be former spouse? Do you want an amicable parting, or a contentious split that drips animosity for years, even decades, to come? Are there children to consider, and what do you want them to remember about the divorce?

You can't set the tone yourself, but you are responsible for at least half. Planning on contesting the divorce terms? Do it in a sane, sensible manner.

Many people hope for an uncontested divorce, a parting in which both people agree on everything involved. It's often a challenge, though, considering these people also decided they could not agree to keep a marriage together.

While often beginning amiably enough, the process can go awry. The voices of friends, ego, pride, jealously, rage and resentment can all intermingle with substantive property decisions. One stray comment, just the wrong words, can destroy the spirit of an uncontested divorce. What started out as a friendly parting becomes contested and expensive.

How do you limit conflict? Simply restrain yourself. Stick to the business of divorce. Too often, one spouse says something awful enough to collapse an agreement that's perfectly reasonable to both parties. Good reasons exist to nullify agreements, but pride and ego can needlessly spin the situation out of control and result in a litigated divorce.

Also, don't consider sharing an attorney. In Georgia, one lawyer may not represent both parties to a divorce. Your attorney has one mission: representing your best interest and no one else's.

CAN YOU REMAIN FRIENDS WITH YOUR SPOUSE?

Decide, in consultation with your attorney, the value of an ongoing friendship with your ex-spouse. Do you want to remain on speaking terms? Or do you just want that person to go away? And how much are you willing to concede to keep him or her happy? Relying on unemotional advice from your lawyer or other marriage expert can prevent a long-lasting mistake.

Assume your spouse is considering his or her best interest, if only for the duration of the divorce. Both of you want to keep assets needed to pay the bills. Cutthroat? Seemingly, but it's also true. In fact, when divorces grow the most heated, as negotiations could end the struggle, the emotional toll is the heaviest.

You may also need to temper feelings when young children are involved. Your spouse will remain the child's parent, forever bonding them. You must, with good council, weigh all of the emotional stress and legal necessities when deciding on the future relationship with a soon-to-be ex-spouse.

TIME TO GATHER INFORMATION

Two-income families represent a modern norm. A divorce must untangle the often-complex paper trail of wages earned, investments made and debts paid. One person may pay the bills, track the bank accounts and handle investments. Maybe it's a matter of shared responsibility. Regardless, a divorce must make it all transparent.

Once you decide to divorce, never allow your spouse to control the documents, because information can make or break a case at trial. Become an information magnet, particularly in the early days of divorce. Even take action while the marriage still works by insisting on a bill-paying partnership. Once the divorce is filed, mutual suspicion makes it trying at best to gather records.

The most relevant items you must gather include three to five years of the following:

- Personal and corporate tax returns
- Checking, savings and money market account statements
- Investment account statements
- Stock and bond certificates
- Financial statements
- Mortgage applications and other information
- Credit card information
- Information on debts and other liabilities
- Long-distance telephone bills
- Cellular telephone bills
- Medical records
- Health insurance policies
- Life insurance policies
- Retirement accounts such as 401Ks and IRAs.

Put this information away for safekeeping, allowing you the option of using it at trial. It may or may not prove pertinent, but you cannot afford to take the risk.

Simply obtaining information, though, does not assure you of winning most of the marital assets in a divorce. Division of assets hinges on the facts of the case. The collected information, however, can protect against a variety of unforeseen outcomes, such as the death or illness of your spouse. Information allows you to exert more control and to know the stakes.

Bank accounts can often lead to enlightening disclosures. They may contain facts and figures known by only one marriage partner. Most employed people get paid twice a month, so the account would include deposits to a checking account, customarily, on the first and 15th day of each month. What if your spouse claims a monthly income of $10,000 but you discover he or she deposits $25,000 into the checking account each month? Maybe it's a large commission, bonus or other money. You need to know the income source, because it could make a huge difference in the division of assets or the amount of child support your spouse might pay.

We'll deal with asset tracing in a later chapter, but you should know it's a delicate skill that can lead to devastatingly effective evidence. Consider long-distance and cellular telephone records. They can establish an illicit relationship with page after page of cellular calls to a certain number.

A lawyer may request both personal and business cellular phone and long-distance records, showing if a spouse is hiding calls behind business accounts. The information could force a guilty spouse to settle a case to keep an employer from learning how he or she spent company time and money.

It's not enough to operate on a hunch, suspecting without the ability to prove misdeeds by a spouse. And proof is the divider between effective or ineffective information. If you can't prove it, don't bring it up. You risk appearing vindictive or deceitful by presenting potentially damaging information without solid proof.

A decision to present evidence must come in the context of the overall strategy of a case.

Seven Simple Steps to Prepare for Divorce

1. Prepare a list of the family's assets and liabilities. Know where to find financial documents and make copies.

2. Start saving money in your own separate bank account, so you will have cash to pay bills. You will have to disclose these funds, but you will have immediate access to them.

3. Decide which assets you would like to keep and which you are willing to relinquish.

4. Do not expect the same lifestyle you enjoyed when you were married. Divorce can be financially devastating to both partners.

5. Apply for credit in your own name so you can start building an individual credit history.

6. Know the divorce laws. Georgia is an equitable division state. Income earned during the marriage is considered marital property but the distribution is not necessarily fifty-fifty.

7. Gather the documents and proof necessary to prove your separate property claims.

Think Strategically

It's important to recognize that in this instance, your spouse is the opposition. It may seem a tough distinction after marriage. Or it may come with ease. It is, however, the reality and like anyone entering any negotiation, it's best to operate from a position of strength. Don't show any weaknesses while gathering information.

Informal negotiations typically initiate the opening moves. Separate your emotions from the practical objective of reaching a settlement on your terms. Use these negotiations to find out what the opposition wants. But never let the opposition know your most prized possession or asset.

You should assume the case is destined for trial. Consider settlement a bonus, not an anticipated, logical outcome. Remember, your own emotions can snarl the process but those of family and friends can irrevocably shatter negotiations. They may talk about what is right, how much you could get, how far you could push and what your other friends have gotten from their divorces.

Be realistic instead. Realize the case depends on evidence and witnesses who can substantiate your claims in court.

A successful financial divorce needs both.

3

With or Without An Attorney

Divorce forces a series of important decisions. How hard should you push? Who should you trust to give you critical advice? With so much at risk, it's critical to structure your divorce properly and choose the methods that lead to the best possible outcome. Mistakes can make it difficult to maintain your lifestyle in the future.

There is a stereotypical image of divorce. Two warring people. Two attorneys. And a judge or jury to sort it all out. In Georgia, the reality is far different. Not all divorces evolve into wars anymore and mediators, often court mandated, and collaborative family attorneys work to create amiable results.

REPRESENTING YOURSELF

Do-it-yourself divorce is on the rise all over the country, and Georgia is no different. Simply, everyone has the right to represent himself or herself in court. Some people may feel they cannot afford an attorney. Others believe their cases are so simple that they don't need an attorney. Others have surfed various divorce websites on the Internet and feel they can handle their affairs as well as a professional.

It's called filing *pro se*, which is Latin for "in one's own behalf." The number of pro se divorces may reach 50% of the total in some Georgia counties. It is particularly common after a short marriage that results in the accumulation of few assets.

Georgia courts do not offer special arrangements or counseling for people who decide to file pro se, but most county courts do provide the necessary forms, often allowing an Internet download. Many fee-based websites offer to assist pro se litigants. Consider this option with caution and make sure the appropriate county court doesn't already provide the forms for free.

The general key for pro se divorce is knowing when to embrace the do-it-yourself approach and when to seek professional help. Pro se litigants risk misunderstanding the rules of court and can inaccurately fill out the forms. They may not know when, or if, they should address the judge or understand the need for evidence in a case. If they are awarded property, do they know how to take possession? You might fail to prove that certain assets are separate property and your spouse could leave the marriage with those assets.

Most judges expect a pro se litigant to know the rules of the court and behave like a lawyer. Neither the judge nor other court officials can offer advice at a hearing. You are on your own, which is a daunting prospect if your spouse chooses to hire a lawyer and you end up confused or frustrated.

In cases of a truly uncontested divorce, involving no children or property, representing yourself may be viable. It's as if a home do-it-yourselfer attempted to re-tile a bathroom. You might get in the middle of this project and regret the decision to tackle it, but it's unlikely to destroy your home.

When filing pro se, you must file the complaint for divorce, which tells the court you wish to end the marriage. This also describes the actions you wish the court to take, such as the division of property.

You must have a copy of the complaint served or given to your spouse. A sheriff or other process server does the job, and there is a fee.

The final steps depend on how your spouse responds to the complaint. No response can lead to the declaration of an uncontested divorce. The court may schedule a hearing if there are matters such as child support or division of property to decide. If the spouse contests the divorce, the court will schedule the case for trial.

The level of difficulty can spike. Filing pro se when children, extensive amounts of property or other complex arrangements are involved can feel like you are performing surgery on yourself. Divorce becomes serious as you heighten the possibility of damaging your future. If you make the decision to represent yourself, you should attend a pro se divorce clinic typically led by legal services organizations or men's and women's rights groups. Often a family law attorney stands by at the clinic to guide you through the process, to teach you how to prepare the necessary documents and answer questions. You are alone, however, when it's time for the final hearing.

BENEFITS OF A SPECIALIST

Approach hiring an attorney as if you are shopping for the most valuable single item you will ever purchase. It's not a time for casual decision. Personalities need to mesh. And the attorney must have the experience and expertise for your specific circumstances.

Most attorneys focus on one or two practice areas, a trend over the last two decades responsible for increasing the number of specialized lawyers. No matter your need, some attorney offers the specific skills to help. More than one million attorneys practice in the United States, nearly 26,000 of them in Georgia.

Start your search by asking friends who have experienced divorce. Ask them for recommendations. If you know attorneys who practice in fields other than matrimonial law, ask them to refer a good family lawyer.

The website of the State Bar of Georgia (www.gabar.org) offers a good resource, particularly the family law section. Marriage counselors and therapists, accountants, financial planners, business managers and clergymen often know family lawyers with outstanding reputations and good track records.

Use all of the sources to narrow the candidates down to just the attorneys whose strengths fit your needs. For example, if you have a business, significant assets or other complex property issues, hire a firm with the capabilities and staff to manage a large asset case.

Regardless of the attorney, the goal should be the same: settlement. If you realistically believe your case may end in court, though, make sure to choose an attorney with a reputation as an effective trial lawyer.

Do not stop with research, because a successful lawyer-client relationship hinges on more than skill. You want someone you will enjoy working with in the months needed to finalize a divorce.

INITIAL INTERVIEWS

After sorting through the qualified candidates, isolate at least two and then schedule initial interviews with them. Seek the most qualified person who fits comfortably with your personality.

Expect to discuss the basic history of the marriage and the issues involved in the divorce. Be candid. Describe the good points and the bad. Lawyers, bound by an ethical obligation, cannot disclose the information you provide without your consent. Also, once an attorney meets with one spouse and hears the marital history, he or she cannot represent the other spouse.

Go prepared at the initial meeting with the following critical information:

- Length of the marriage
- Names and ages of children and any special needs
- Fault of either spouse
- Each party's relationship with the children and child care responsibilities
- Income of each party
- Work history of each party
- Summary of assets and debts

The lawyer may ask for a detailed timeline and summary of the marital history after the initial interview. Expect to report each and every issue your spouse could bring up during the case. No attorney can correctly evaluate the case unless you present all the facts on both sides.

QUESTIONS TO ASK YOUR ATTORNEY

"Do you charge for the initial interview?"

Some lawyers offer a free initial consultation, but most matrimonial lawyers charge for the first visit, typically the attorney's hourly rate of from $150 to several hundred dollars.

If you hire the attorney at the initial visit, the consultation fee usually is paid from the retainer.

"How do you charge for your services?"

Expect to pay a family lawyer based on an hourly rate, including work performed by paralegals. Be smart. Choose an attorney who can meet your expectations at a price you can afford. Charges include each meeting with your lawyer, time spent on the phone as well as the time the office staff works on the case. Don't be shy. Make sure you understand how the lawyer bills.

"Do I sign a fee agreement?"

When you make a decision to hire, most lawyers will execute a written fee agreement. Review the document and understand the billing procedures and the other costs. Determine the amount and payment date of the initial retainer, an advance payment for time and expenses. The lawyer typically bills against this retainer each month for work performed on your behalf.

Most lawyers believe, as we do, that unused retainers should be refundable. For example, a client may sign a fee agreement providing a $10,000 retainer. Then, let's say the couple reconciles, the case is finalized or the client opts to use another lawyer after the original attorney bills only $7,000. The client usually receives the remaining $3,000, but the original agreement should make this provision clear. Make sure you understand the fee agreement.

Remember, the initial retainer is a beginning and may not cover the complete divorce. The fee agreement should address supplemental retainers throughout the case. A large-asset case or a hotly contested case may require the client to supplement the retainer several times during the divorce.

Make sure the agreement details expenses obligated to the client, such as long-distance charges, subpoena fees and photocopy and fax charges. The fee agreement may also address payment details if the court requires one spouse to pay the other's legal fees.

A few lawyers will offer flat-fee divorces. Consider this option carefully. Review documents and services available through the courts and local agencies. Know what you are buying and make sure the flat rate doesn't simply provide services already available at low-cost or free.

A divorce with many financial and emotional components may generate tremendous expense, enough to shock some. Fees in a divorce billed on an hourly basis can range from several thousand dollars to more than a hundred thousand dollars, depending on the assets, issues and the personalities involved.

Many large-asset cases require the attention of two or more lawyers. One lawyer may concentrate on the facts of the marriage and the witnesses to those facts while another lawyer works specifically on assets and business issues related to the case.

Most family lawyers in Georgia operate alone. Weigh your needs against their capabilities and willingness to bring in assistance when needed. Consider if the facts of your situation, such as large assets or complex custody issues, might require the resources of a larger firm. In such a case, one attorney might focus on the history of a 20-year marriage with three children and a spouse with an addiction problem. Another attorney might concentrate on the financial terms, conditions and history of a successful multimillion-dollar business. Do your homework and make sure the lawyer you choose meets your specific needs and, therefore, can handle your case.

Also, if your case involves significant assets, debts or other complications, make certain your lawyer has the necessary experience and time to prepare your case. You've lived it, and you know everything about your case. Your attorney is probably very interested in the facts of your case, but you must bring the lawyer up to speed so that he or she may either negotiate a settlement or try the case, explaining all the details to the judge or jury.

"Do you send out monthly statements?"

Monitor the charges incurred in your case on a regular basis. Lawyers and staff members must compile a lot of information to prepare your case for trial. Even if you don't talk to the lawyer regularly, work is probably being done on your behalf.

Use your lawyer's time wisely. If you use the law firm as a daily emotional counseling service, your bill will increase dramatically. Attorneys and paralegals at most firms record their time daily. Monthly statements inform the client about the billing charges incurred and the work that generated those charges. We ask clients to review our monthly statements and call with any questions.

"How long will my case take?"

Settling a divorce generally takes less time than litigating. A case that goes to trial could take a year to 18 months from start to finish. Intricate cases with delays and obstructions can take longer than two years to resolve. If you face litigation, count on a year or more of preparation and delay until you have your divorce. Blame for delays falls on the large number of divorce cases in the court system as well as the effort required to determine the assets and other issues involved.

If your spouse fails to provide financial records, you may have to subpoena those records or get a court order to obtain them. In these instances, your case will take longer to resolve than if both sides put all the information on the table. If you must provide audits and detailed financial examinations of the assets and values of the businesses involved, take into account the scheduling and availability of other professionals.

The path to a long, expensive divorce begins when you, your spouse or the other lawyer decide to battle every detail of a case. Many cases start out as litigated matters while tempers and emotions run high. Sometimes, mounting fees calm those emotions and allow a settlement.

Most attorneys try to determine the assets, debts and other significant issues involved and proceed down the path of settlement in each case. Some cases, though, must litigate because the other side simply will not settle. A judge's ruling can resolve the case more quickly and reasonably than expecting the parties to resolve their differences themselves.

"What do you expect of me?"

Ask the lawyer what he or she needs from you. Expect to do some work yourself, obtaining and developing information your attorney needs to fully explain the case. Fee agreements often explain a client's responsibilities and emphasize the importance of cooperation. In fact, many firms reserve the right to withdraw from a case if a client is dishonest or refuses to help prepare critical information. Remember, it's in your best interest to help, and you and your attorney should work together for the same goal. Return calls from your attorney quickly. Provide requested information in a timely manner. A client thoroughly involved in the preparation and details of the case becomes more informed and is always happier with the result.

YES TO EXPERIENCE, NO TO GUARANTEES

No attorney can guarantee a certain outcome. An experienced family law specialist can explain the range of possible outcomes. A good attorney can evaluate your case and explain to you how a judge or jury might react.

4

Alternative Dispute Resolution

Family law experts frustrated with the destructive nature of divorce litigation have developed several new approaches to settlement of family law issues over the past two decades. In the 1990s, they developed a process known as collaborative law. The shift represented a radical departure from the more adversarial way of ending a marriage. By that time, many county courts in Georgia had already turned to mediation, in which an independent mediator works to conclude a divorce outside the courtroom.

Many courts, with each county setting its own rules, require mediation. Choosing a collaborative law approach, meanwhile, is the choice of the parties involved. Understanding the distinctions between the two approaches is critical for anyone considering a divorce in Georgia.

NEW REALITIES: MEDIATION AND COLLABORATIVE LAW

Most courts that hear divorce cases in the Atlanta metropolitan counties refer the parties to mediation at some point in the process, but there is no statewide standard. Fulton County, for example, relies on in-house mediators and pays the expenses for the first several hours. Cobb County provides a list of mediators, requiring you to choose one and pay the mediator an hourly rate from your own pocket.

Regardless of the details, a judge's order requiring mediation is increasingly unavoidable. If mediation seems inevitable, it is possible for the attorneys to agree on a mediator and hire him or her privately.

"In mediation, each side agrees upon the person who will facilitate the negotiation," says Susan Hurst, a family and collaborative law attorney in Atlanta. "That neutral person is there for the mediation and his or her only involvement is settlement of the case. A mediator's only loyalty is to the idea of settlement and keeping people out of the courtroom."

Mediators approach each case by considering the outcome if the divorce goes to trial. While the process might keep a divorce from proceeding before a judge, there is no guarantee that mediation will result in either a more equitable or less equitable outcome for the parties involved. And if mediation fails, trial remains an option.

Collaborative law, meanwhile, represents a complete paradigm shift in the way divorcing people relate to each other and attorneys relate to the parties.

In collaborative practice, the parties and their lawyers sign a participation agreement stating they all agree to work out of court. The goal is to settle the case, and abandoning the process requires the parties to fire their lawyers and seek new counsel.

"The mentality of the collaborative process is that the best resolution to a family divorce is for all of the parties' interests to be considered and served, as much as possible, by all of the players," Hurst says. "It is collaborative. While I may be an advocate for my clients' interest, I might also be an advocate for all of the family and all of the interests being met."

Through a series of face-to-face settlement sessions, the clients and attorneys work toward agreement on all the issues involved in a divorce. Their goal is to reduce the level of hostility and produce a settlement that maximizes assets and relationships. Divorcing people who want to continue relationships with their ex-spouses are most likely to use collaborative law. This includes couples with children, those who own or operate a family business, people who share the same workplace and those who have the same large group of friends and don't want to lose any of them in the divorce.

"Most importantly, it can allow people to let go of the vitriolic anger," Hurst says. "I have seen people come into a negotiation unable to speak to each other and by the end of the day they hug."

Attorneys Must Withdraw If Settlement Fails

The unique agreement at the outset regarding the conduct and structure of negotiations differentiates collaborative law from mediation and litigation. The structure also gives powerful incentives for attorneys to successfully reach a conclusion. If the case does not settle and the divorce goes to court, both collaborative lawyers must withdraw from the case. The requirement offers powerful protections. The collaborative process requires everyone to comfortably discuss the facts of the case, and participants would not feel safe sharing personal information with an attorney on the other side who could wind up deposing or cross-examining them in court.

Attorneys in litigated divorces—especially those involving wealthy litigants—are occasionally accused of sabotaging settlements so the attorneys can justify taking a case to court. Attorney fees in these contentious cases can be significant. The poison pill feature of collaborative law removes any incentive attorneys might have to stretch out the divorce and increase fees.

In the short term, collaborative law can save money. The sensible approach to divorce has an even greater potential to set divorcing couples on a long-term path to financial security.

Some collaborative lawyers practice in groups of independent, unaffiliated legal professionals, because two attorneys trained in collaborative law do the best job handling collaborative cases. Many of these practice groups utilize a team approach, bringing in family therapists, financial planners, CPAs, estate planners and other professionals, when needed, to organize the finances of the parties and help them begin their new lives.

LOCATE A COLLABORATIVE LAWYER

Attorneys practicing collaborative law operate in most Georgia urban areas. You are less likely to find a local group if you live in a small town or rural area of the state. If you are interested in exploring the possibility of a collaborative law divorce, check out the websites for the International Academy of Collaborative Professionals (www.collaborativepractice.com) to find a collaboratively trained family attorney in your area.

Not all lawyers who handle cases collaboratively are members of practice groups, so you should ask if a certain attorney handles cases in this manner.

S N A P S H O T

A More Humane Method

His View

Most evenings, he welcomed any excuse to stay late at work and avoid dinner with her. To him, she was a wife who never really listened. She just didn't seem to care.

Ten years of their marriage was about five years too long. Young and in love in the beginning, they tackled life's milestones with an ease their friends envied. They were best friends who led charmed lives, especially in financial matters. Investments paid off handsomely. They rarely fought, or even disagreed. A perfect couple.

Over time, though, they drifted apart. He missed the days she doted over him. Without arguing or screaming, he decided to take his life back. He anticipated a messy divorce, not because of any animosity but because of their latest financial venture. They invested in a start-up company, a fragile newcomer easily destroyed by an ownership in crisis.

Worried about their two children, the relationship with his wife and the health of the new company, he talked to a recently divorced colleague. The colleague suggested an attorney who practices mostly in collaborative law. He set up an appointment. He was nervous, not sure of the best decision, but for his own happiness he wanted to explore this option.

When the attorney questioned him about his priorities, he listed his children, his happiness, friendship with his wife and his new business venture. Designed to keep the divorce out of litigation, collaborative law could help him preserve the important things, both emotionally and financially. He took brochures and other information and agreed to discuss collaborative law with her.

Her View

For her, the marriage had also changed. She remembered a happy, unpredictable husband from early in their marriage. After their children were born, she noticed his spark and enthusiasm for life melting away.

She once pampered him, relying on strong maternal feelings to make him happy. When she said it was time to start a family, he stalled until she agreed on just one child.

He wasn't as happy as she was about their young son, but he seemed to grow accustomed to parenthood. Nine months later, without any thought or planning, she discovered she was pregnant again. He wasn't thrilled. After the birth of their daughter, she could not believe how much time and energy two small children consumed.

Gradually he seemed more and more uncomfortable at home. He never talked about his job, preferring to spend free time watching TV or playing video games.

She knew they were drifting apart. She knew he was unhappy. But she was blindsided when he came home talking about a divorce. She suggested marriage counseling, but he said counseling could not heal his feelings. If he couldn't feel right with her, he just wanted to be alone. She could only nod as he explained how they could dissolve the marriage without a messy confrontation.

The Result

They chose a collaborative law divorce designed to save their friendship, protect their children from the heartache of a drawn-out ordeal and allow them to retain their considerable assets. Once she selected a collaborative law divorce, her attorney called his attorney to arrange the first joint session.

They met at her attorney's office. Realizing she was nervous and unsure of the process, he tried to give her as much control of the session as possible. The meeting started with a short introduction and a reading of the collaborative law participation agreement. The attorneys asked for any general questions on the process. The attorneys explained that the process would take at least 30 days, since the state of Georgia requires that a divorce petition be on file for that long before finalization. Many divorces take longer, which is no one's fault. Everyone agreed to work one session at a time until they resolved everything and the court could sign the final decree.

They agreed the sessions would determine the best arrangement for their children, divide property and possibly designate alimony. The attorneys made it clear that hashing out marital disagreements was usually not productive. Both attorneys suggested that a mental health professional attend the meetings, and they asked the couple to consider therapy to work through any unresolved issues before continuing.

They worked through several sessions as well as meeting regularly with the family therapist. It was all painful but civilized. They decided she should have primary custody of the children, with each of them designating specific days of possession. He would retain ownership of the new company and she would get their home. He kept his retirement accounts, agreeing to pay her substantial maintenance payments over time that gave her 58% of their assets.

Emotions often ran high.

When he asked to have the children half the summer, she broke down and stormed out of the session. When they discussed their home, she sobbed but regained her composure. The weekend after they finalized an agreement about visitation, he got confused about time and brought the children home late on Sunday night.

While she was upset, they worked through it. He gave her as much latitude as possible, particularly after his attorney explained that she was not as far along in the process of disengagement as he was.

The final session was their longest one. They finalized the house agreement, ownership of the new business interest as well as child custody and child support agreements. Without much conflict they divvied up the rest of the household items and the little shared debt. With the final session winding down, neither could believe they were still talking to one another.

5

Strategies to Save Money on Legal Fees

A client willing to tell a lawyer to just win at any cost often makes a lasting mistake. Some lawyers have been accused of churning fees, recognizing their client is excitable and possibly hopeful of taking out a dose of vengeance. A paperwork blizzard can result, with the lawyer issuing numerous motions and demanding detailed depositions. The moves can eat through retainers at a furious pace.

Other attorneys, often the best attorneys, take the time to tell clients the what, where and how. They want the client to understand specific actions. That said, never assume. Always ask questions and make sure you understand the way your attorney spends your money.

Never incur an expense to get information you already have or can get in a less expensive or confrontational way. For example, your attorney may opt to depose your spouse to learn the location

60

of a specific asset, but you can't afford to assume this is just standard procedure. What if you know where the asset is, but you never informed your attorney? It's the type of oversight that can cause an unneeded deposition and cost you cash.

If your attorney fails to discuss the reasoning for a certain action, don't hesitate to ask.

Asking "Why are we deposing my ex?" may seem dumb, something you should know without asking. But asking the question may help you avoid an expensive mistake. Also, questions can educate you about the process, knowledge you can use throughout the divorce to avoid breaking the bank.

CONTINGENCY FEES

The disciplinary rules of the State Bar of Georgia state that contingent fee arrangements in divorce cases are improper. While contingency fees are common in some civil actions, the unique set of very human relationships in divorce cases creates problems for this system. Personal injury lawyers may advertise that you don't pay "unless we collect." If a payday comes, the attorney claims one-third to one-half of any award or settlement, plus the cost of the case. The client receives the remainder.

In Georgia, this approach is deemed unsuitable for divorce because it can create a possible conflict of interest between the lawyer and the client. An attorney should not pressure a client to accept an inadequate settlement so the attorney can get paid.

Similarly, allowing contingency fees would raise questions in the valuation of non-cash assets, with high values earning the lawyer a larger cut.

An exception occurs after the divorce, if an attorney is hired to collect past due alimony or child support. The lawyer should agree to a contingency fee only if it is the sole economically feasible way a client can afford representation. The fee must also be reasonable as defined by the state's ethical guidelines.

10 Effective Strategies for Controlling Legal Fees

Never forget the meter is running. Each time a lawyer, paralegal or anyone else associated with a firm works on your case, they will bill for their time. You must take responsibility for controlling legal fees by adhering to the following strategies:

1. Let your attorney know from the start that money is an issue.

2. Be aware that it costs you money each time you meet with your attorney, talk to the attorney on the telephone or have staff members working on your behalf.

3. Never use your attorney or the staff as a counseling service. This can be very expensive.

4. Help your attorney collect financial information, track down documents and do other work he or she would have to pay someone to do and you can do easily.

5. Don't be afraid of a friendly reminder. Each time during the divorce that you do anything designed to keep your fees down, tell your attorney what you are doing.

6. Distinguish a real emergency from the panic of divorce. Emergency calls to your attorney after hours and on weekends can cost you a lot of money.

7. Don't encourage (or allow) your attorney to secure an asset worth less than the cost of acquiring it.

8. Let your attorney know which assets are important to you and which are not. It's expensive to fight on too many fronts.

9. If you feel you can settle certain sticky issues on your own, such as custody of your children or who should run a family business, do so with your attorney's advice.

10. Never tell your attorney to do whatever it takes. This is the same as saying you don't care how much it costs.

6

Work Toward Settlement

After a divorce, you will probably tell someone that you were taken to the cleaners by an unfair settlement. Often both parties to the divorce make that claim, a contention that's common as a plot device in movies, television and books.

Studies show that people who take an active role in the settlement of their cases, rather than going to court and having a judge or jury decide the outcome, feel better about their divorces. Settlements in which both sides give some and take some are preferable to almost any court verdict.

WHAT IS FAIR?

Parties to a divorce often confuse the equal distribution of assets with fairness. Georgia law considers all property acquired during a marriage as marital property, except for inheritance and gifts from third parties. The property should be divided equitably, but there is neither a legal guarantee of a fifty-fifty split nor a formula to calculate the division. Awards could grant one spouse almost nothing and the other almost everything, although some judges and juries begin by considering fairly equal divisions, depending on the facts of a particular case.

A judge or jury can weigh several factors when considering an award, including:

- The duration of marriage
- Prior marriage of either spouse
- The age, health and occupation of each spouse
- Vocational skills and employability
- Contribution to the family and the amount and sources of income
- Debts and liabilities
- The award of alimony
- The opportunities of each spouse for future assets or income

When weighing these factors, a judge will find few couples absolutely equal. Consider a couple married for many years and near retirement. The wife never worked outside the home, they have no assets maturing in the future and the man had an affair. In an instance such as this, the wife might get more of the assets than her husband if she does not receive alimony.

MAJOR FINANCIAL BLUNDERS

An experienced lawyer, often with the help of a valuation expert, can provide you with information to help determine the worth of your marital assets. You must decide which assets are worth a fight.

Too often, people in a divorce make the following major financial blunders:

- Incorrectly valuing a closely held business
- Failing to consider the tax effect of certain assets
- Being unaware that retirement accounts, stock options, deferred compensation plans and accrued bonuses can be divided between the parties
- Failing to consider the debts in a marriage

Clients and their attorneys also make many smaller mistakes. For instance, it's easy to forget about such assets as frequent flyer miles or the value of points you receive from using certain credit cards. They overlook tax prepayments, tax loss carry forwards and employee stock options or fail to realize when one party prepays a debt from community funds on an asset that is separate property.

MOST CASES SETTLE

Remember, your best interest is almost always best served by working out an amicable division of property rather than giving away the responsibility for your future to a judge or jury. You know what is important to you and you can be very specific. A judge doesn't really want the task of dividing your property and may even resent the time it takes. The result can be a quick division that ends the case, but which does not consider any sentimental attachments to specific items.

Even if you go to court over more significant issues, you can divide personal property prior to trial and eliminate some points a judge must consider. Sometimes the meaning of a specific piece of personal property far outweighs its value. In one case, child custody brought the parties into court. With that issue resolved, all that remained was possession of a vintage automobile the man cherished, and the woman fought him over it for months. Without that battle, the parents and children could have begun to heal from the divorce months earlier.

THE IMPORTANCE OF MEDIATION

Mediation has affected more people than any other feature of family law in the past quarter century. Most counties in Georgia now require some form of mediation to limit the number of divorce cases that wind up before a judge.

Moving the divorce away from the courthouse and into the mediator's office can often reduce the inherent adversarial tension. The job of a divorce lawyer in court is to win for the client. The job of a mediator is to provide a reality check, helping each client understand how a court might divide property and the benefits of an out-of-court settlement negotiated to best meet his or her needs.

"It's an opportunity for the parties to control their case," says Nancy Grossman, a senior staff attorney and mediator for Fulton County Superior Court. "It's an opportunity for them to have some input into resolving their issues and an alternative to a judge deciding their case for them."

The approach varies between mediators. Some prefer a passive role, simply acting as a go-between. Others take a more aggressive tact, actively working with the parties to forge an agreement. No one standard exists. In fact, not all mediators are lawyers. It is possible to become certified as a mediator by the Georgia Office of Dispute Resolution after completing specific training. Some lawyers, though, mediate divorces without the certification. Your attorney can find the mediator who provides the approach that best fits your needs.

Grossman, who is certified, sees her role clearly. "I'm there to help them understand the reality if it goes go to court. I make sure they understand that if they go to court they could lose so much more, and I ask them to weigh that risk against finding something in the middle."

The actual structure of the mediation proceedings varies according to the mediator, with some preferring face-to-face negotiations. Others gather attorneys and their clients in one room to hear the ground rules before separating, with the mediator shuttling from room to room to negotiate. Mediators such as M.T. Simmons of Atlanta believe the two parties should be separated as he works to negotiate a settlement.

About 80% to 90% of all mediated cases settle, which lightens the load in busy courthouses and often leads to less acrimonious divisions of property. Simmons, who often mediates divorces with property valuing millions of dollars, says the system works even in an acrimonious split. And often attorneys depend on the mediator to create momentum.

"A good many of the people are ready to settle, but I can almost tell when it starts if they're not," he says. "They're not psychologically ready and their attorneys are looking for the mediator to bring them to a conclusion."

Mediators offer a powerful incentive, providing hope of reaching an equitable agreement without risking everything in a trial with no guarantee of success. No matter what a lawyer may expect as an outcome, the courtroom can surprise. Unpleasantly surprise.

For Simmons, the key is reality testing. He prefers working with the findings of forensic accountants, who provide fine details of a couple's finances. Armed with specifics, he helps the parties negotiate. For example, one spouse might receive many dollars worth of property and still want alimony. Simmons works with clients to understand the reality that they can live well without the alimony. "In the final analysis, they should listen to the lawyers and understand they might not get more by going before a judge or jury," he says.

The duration of mediation sessions is often based on the size of the assets involved. Two or three hours of mediation might end a pro se divorce with relatively few assets. More complex cases might require a full day to negotiate, but most mediators try to complete the job in one session.

THE BENEFITS ARE SIGNIFICANT

Legal fees for a warring middle-class couple can race into the six-figure range and a divorce can take the span of a presidential administration to finalize. Mediation can short-circuit that schedule at a much lower price.

The major benefit of mediation may be to lower the level of hostility inherent in a divorce. Even when mediation fails to resolve all the differences, just the act of dealing with each other in a controlled environment and reaching agreement on some issues can reduce the amount of animosity, along with the expense.

Mediation often brings the first jarring measure of reality. "It's always very emotional," Grossman says. "One party doesn't want divorce, while the other party has moved ahead. They often want to know what the court might do, particularly with alimony."

With an experienced mediator, though, both parties can feel confident in the end result and know they guaranteed an equitable outcome rather than taking the risk of going to court.

BEWARE OF MEDIATION ABUSE

Critics of mediation often ask questions about perceived weaknesses in the system. For instance, what prevents someone from underestimating or hiding assets?

A party who hides something or otherwise negotiates in bad faith can abuse the mediation process. The theory behind mediation is sound and your attorney should protect you from those abuses.

Ideally, discovery is completed prior to mediation and you should have the opportunity to determine the value and character of all assets.

Mediations can break down because of disagreements over values, particularly in the case of a closely held business. For example, a man who ran a paper company and wanted to continue running it after the divorce valued the business at $2 million. His soon-to-be ex-wife valued the same company at $17 million. He wanted to give her other assets worth $1 million for her half of the company's value. She wanted half the value her side gave the company, or $8.5 million. Each party brought a business valuation expert to court to justify the numbers. With no one willing to budge, there was nowhere to go but the courthouse.

Some people, in a rush to reach a settlement, might negotiate without enough information and accept a bad division of property. In the past, some women's rights groups have questioned the value of mediation for this reason. With mediation becoming a standard process, women are now seen as being on equal ground during a mediation and capable of negotiating fair settlements.

The bottom line? We've seen clients go into the process skeptical of the other side's motives and still come out with a worthwhile settlement.

YOUR ATTORNEY'S ROLE IN RESOLVING DISPUTES

In a contested divorce, your attorney should provide you with fair, aggressive advocacy to allow you and your spouse to reach a negotiated settlement. If the other side makes unreasonable demands, however, the attorney must be willing to go to trial.

Expect your attorney to give you a realistic evaluation of the case. Pouring money into extensive litigation is not likely to give you a substantially lopsided property division. If you reject reasonable goals and demand an unreasonable property settlement, the costs will rise.

Conversely, if you are so distraught or exasperated that you are willing to accept almost any settlement offer, your attorney should be the voice of reason. You should focus on the long-term effects of the outcome.

Your attorney should consider the following questions when advising you whether to settle or try your case:

- Will facts harmful to you be revealed at trial?
- Will the parties make credible witnesses?
- Will the other witnesses be credible?
- Will expert testimony be necessary and at what cost?
- Who is the opposing attorney and how much experience in these cases does he or she have?
- Will the law or the facts of your case be difficult to explain to a jury?
- What county will the case be tried in and will its local rules or juror pool put the client at a disadvantage?
- What judge will try the case?
- Are there any problems with the admissibility of important evidence?
- Can your separate property assets be traced adequately?

Your attorney should be able to use the answers to these questions to determine a fair resolution of the case, since he or she approaches the problem without your emotional involvement.

7

Coping With Temporary Matters

For many people, the most chaotic time of ending a marriage comes immediately following the filing of the divorce petition. The one who chooses to divorce (or if the decision is mutual) is usually better prepared for the challenges. If you aren't prepared, though, expect a measure of chaos. Are you the one who normally pays the bills and keeps close tabs on the money? If not, you may find yourself lacking the resources for a comfortable life during the divorce. Hopefully, you're ready to cope.

Couples in a functioning relationship support each other. They pay the bills. They buy groceries. They budget for incidentals. Divorce, though, creates dysfunction. Some spouses completely disregard the welfare of their life-long partners. One spouse might move on, abandoning the other emotionally and financially. If you're left behind, ask your attorney to seek help on your

72

behalf. They can often negotiate temporary relief through the court system.

TEMPORARY ORDERS

In about half of all Georgia counties, including Atlanta's Fulton County, a divorce filing automatically triggers the issuance of standing orders setting rules that limit spending and the transfer of funds (except in the ordinary course of business) for necessary items such as mortgage and household bills. Judges in counties lacking the automatic provision typically issue similar orders when requested by an attorney.

Don't assume, though, that an order of the court will end every dispute. It's common for attorneys to disagree about what constitutes ordinary or reasonable expenditures.

In fact, these issues can lead to heated debate. Negotiations preceding settlement or decisions by the court are often required to end disputes over the extent of spending limitations.

While a court order may not end arguments about the details, willful violations can bring serious repercussions, including a contempt of court charge and the possibility of fines.

One of the most serious areas of these orders, and something Georgia judges take very seriously, involves children. The orders typically prevent either parent from removing a child from the court's jurisdiction until the divorce concludes.

While orders granting temporary relief often limit an individual's actions, they can also tell someone the actions that must be done:

- Inventory all property
- Pay temporary child support
- Pay interim attorney fees
- Pay temporary spousal support

- Award use of property, including homes and automobiles
- Operate a family business
- Divide debts
- Provide visitation with children
- Produce documents
- Determine temporary custody and visitation.

TEMPORARY RESTRAINING ORDERS

Where there is the threat of family violence, a court can issue a temporary restraining order. Typically this order is produced by the court at the request of one party to the divorce and it can create broad restrictions.

These orders can demand the end to any violent or harassing actions, grant the possession of a household to one spouse, exclude the other spouse from the home or require one person to provide suitable alternative housing for the other.

Children are also protected. These orders can award temporary child custody, set temporary visitation rights and determine payments for child or spousal support.

The sheriff of the county where the order is issued retains a copy on file for the order's duration, as long as one year. In some instances, and after a hearing, a court will choose to extend the temporary order for as long as three years or even make it permanent. And while filed in the county where the order originates, it is valid throughout Georgia.

TO HER A DRUNK, TO HIM A LOVING DAD

His View

He came home just like any other evening, but he found an empty house. She had left. And she took the kids. He tried to call but she wouldn't answer her cell phone. Eventually, she'd come home, he thought. She had before.

Usually trouble started after he spent a night watching football or baseball with the guys, and she always showed up again after she ran out of money. This time, he wasn't sure he cared. She lectured him about responsibilities. He paid the bills, but she couldn't understand that he just needed to blow off some steam after a long day at work.

And she bugged him about drinking. He knew he didn't have a problem. After all, problem drinkers get drunk at work or start drinking first thing in the morning. He didn't. Besides, it was her problem. She just got more uptight the longer they were married.

Sure, a few times he drank too much, especially when they were out with friends. She said he embarrassed her. He hated going to dinner with those people anyway.

Their arguments escalated after he was passed over for a promotion at work, and a few beers at night allowed him to forget how much he hated his job. She kept saying he drank too much and took his frustrations out on her and the children.

So, he quit drinking at home. Friends and a favorite bar were better anyway. But she complained about that. And, when she started griping, he found it more difficult to control his temper.

This time, though, was different. Days passed after she left and didn't call. He started searching for her, but none of her friends would say anything.

Then he received divorce papers, including a temporary restraining order and an order keeping him away from her and the children. Was she crazy? He'd never been violent with her or the kids.

Her View

She remembered that when she was a child, her father came home every night and drank beer before falling asleep in front of the TV. A grown man passing out in his favorite chair wasn't new to her, but her father was a mellow drunk. Her husband was not.

When they went out with friends, her husband got loud and annoyed everyone. Eventually, their friends, mostly her friends, quit calling. And she was tired of explaining his behavior.

He masked his frustration over his job, never opening up. He was destroying the family. When the children heard his car pull into the driveway, they disappeared into their bedrooms.

She was sympathetic, to a point. She understood he hated his job and was disappointed about a promotion that never happened. When she suggested they attend family therapy, he refused. How do you help someone who refuses all help?

She felt him pull away, and she worried that one evening he would lose his temper and hurt someone. Asking him to stop drinking around her or the children just started the fight all over again. He shoved her against the wall, screamed in her face and raised his fist.

The thought of leaving him scared her. She didn't know if she could raise the children by herself. But she was tired of living in fear.

After he nearly hit her, she took the children. She decided to settle in with her sister and contact a lawyer. She hired a family law attorney and confided that she feared her husband would violently oppose the divorce.

Could they do anything to keep him away from her and the children? She considered him a threat to her safety, and over time she only became more frightened.

The Result

Her attorney asked a judge to issue a protective order. After a hearing, the judge granted her temporary child and spousal support and attorney's fees. She received temporary primary custody of the children and the house during the divorce. He was awarded standard visitation with the children.

He understood the message. This was a serious and disheartening end to their marriage.

8

Short-Term Finances

Georgia courts offer ways to protect the short-term finances of anyone involved in a divorce. The court, however,
cannot end animosity or the need to carefully consider financial
decisions as your attorney works toward a resolution.

A court order can prevent either spouse from improperly raid-
ing joint accounts or running up unnecessary debt. While some
county courts automatically issue such orders, others respond
only to an attorney's request.

The order can limit situations that seem like financial retalia-
tion, such as one spouse blocking access to money for a mortgage
or a car payment. In such an instance, judges react swiftly. They
can declare the offending spouse in contempt of court and fine or
even incarcerate the offender.

While the court system may provide a safety net, be prepared
for the opposing attorney to scrutinize your financial moves.

Use of Joint Accounts

You can legally take money from a joint account or obtain a cash advance from a joint credit card if you are a signatory on the account. But you can expect questions about your motives. Always keep detailed records of any money spent from these accounts. Judges understand purchases for groceries, rent or other essentials. Buying jewelry or taking a business trip to Las Vegas will almost always draw scrutiny.

Joint Credit Card Debt

A divorce cannot make debt disappear. People sometimes believe they can end headaches over a joint credit card account by simply closing the account. Unfortunately, the balance must be paid before the account is actually closed. If you cannot immediately pay off and close the account, consider possible solutions:

- Agree with your spouse to use joint funds to pay off the debt. Then, close the account.
- Apply for a separate credit card for each of you, splitting the balance between the two accounts.
- If your spouse cannot qualify for credit alone, ask a relative or friend to co-sign for a new card. Then, transfer part of the balance.

Paying Bills During the Divorce

Try your best to reach an agreement about which party will pay particular debts. If an agreement is impossible, the court may have to decide who takes responsibility for specific bills. Remember, the failure of your spouse to pay an assigned bill does not free you of responsibility for that debt. Your name remains on the note or credit account, and the lender can still come after you to pay the debt.

The court cannot order a mortgage company or other lender to end a borrower's responsibility. Your contract with the creditor predates the court proceeding, and a divorce does not end the obligation.

9

Discovery

Marriage does not mean a man and woman truly know everything about one another. A divorce can shed light on new facets of the relationship and produce a wealth of new, even unexpected, information.

The process of uncovering this information is called discovery, common in most civil lawsuits, including divorces. Discovery allows the gathering and disclosure of information, often financial, before mediation or trial. Discovery should allow equal and fair negotiations during settlement talks and, if a divorce goes to trial, limit ambush-style surprises.

Discovery can require both spouses to not only produce documents and records but also respond to questions both orally and in writing. Depending on the lawyers, the circumstances and the relationship between the divorcing couple, discovery may be relatively informal or extraordinarily serious and detailed. A spirit of cooperation can reduce the time required and the cost of the case. Throughout discovery, your attorney should always protect your interests, demanding critical information from the other side while making certain that the demands on you are reasonable and within the norms of the court.

As a result, you should understand and follow the discovery process. Schedule strategy sessions with your attorney so you understand the information being sought and why you are seeking it.

HIDING MONEY, FINDING ASSETS

Could your spouse hide assets normally covered in a divorce settlement? Concealing assets isn't easy when digital information allows the tracking of myriad financial details. If a marriage truly reaches meltdown, though, a disgruntled soon-to-be-ex-spouse might make the attempt.

People usually don't get very creative when deciding a hiding place. It's generally more about panicked efforts, not offshore bank accounts. And discovery usually uncovers those clumsy attempts to conceal assets.

Still, you and your attorney should make every effort to confirm that your spouse conceals nothing. You are always better off discovering chicanery while negotiating the divorce.

You may have hope if you uncover the property after the fact. If you discover hidden assets, you may have certain avenues of relief, unless there is a catch-all provision in your divorce decree. For example, if your spouse is awarded all bank accounts in his or her name, discovering an account later won't help you. If your spouse signed, under oath, an inventory detailing a list of accounts, you may be able to lay claim to the newly found assets. You can also place a penalty clause in your divorce decree awarding any undisclosed assets to the other spouse.

Here are some ways people attempt to hide assets:

- Pay off a phony debt to a friend or relative.
- Pay expenses for a girlfriend or boyfriend, such as college tuition, gifts, travel and rent.
- Delay bonuses, stock options, raises or other employment benefits until after the divorce.
- Set up a custodial account in the name of a child who will be your dependent.
- Skim cash from a business he or she owns.
- Pay salary to a nonexistent employee.
- Pay money from the business to a friend or family member for services never rendered, expecting the money to be given back after the divorce.
- For a business owner, delay signing long-term contracts until after the divorce.
- Fail to report the loss of antiques, artwork, hobby equipment, gun collections and tools recently purchased.

PREPARE AN INVENTORY

Keep a record of assets by investigating your personal and business finances before filing for divorce. Make copies of important documents such as several years worth of tax returns, bank account statements and pay stubs. Track anything reflecting joint assets or debts.

Keep these documents in a safe deposit box or, if you still live with your spouse, at a friend's house. Remember to check the tax returns for any loss carry forwards, which often have great value and should be part of the settlement negotiations.

Try to inventory your marital assets before the heat of divorce. List the most valuable assets and take photos if possible. Most cases require a domestic relations financial affidavit, which itemizes assets and debts.

Formal Discovery

Discovery creates a foundation of information necessary to negotiate a fair and accurate settlement or prepare the best case for trial. Several tools allow you and your attorney to dig deeply into issues such as finances and the causes of divorce:

INTERROGATORIES — These are written questions, which must be answered truthfully. Questions can relate to you or your spouse's employment and salary information, bank accounts, charge accounts, assets and debts. A question may ask who else has knowledge of the facts of a case. Interrogatories, usually issued early in the process, can catch people off-guard if they're unaware of an answer's consequences.

You may have to answer these questions yourself. Discuss the interrogatories with your attorney to determine the best response.

REQUEST FOR PRODUCTION OF DOCUMENTS — An attorney can demand specific documents needed to prepare a case. It's common to seek two to five years of bank statements, tax returns, charge statements, business records, insurance information and financial data. Also, the request can include documents supporting separate property claims and any evidence the other party plans to use at trial.

If you fail to produce a document when requested, you generally cannot use that document yourself in court. At trial, your attorney should object to admission of any documents the other side did not produce in time for your attorney to examine them.

REQUEST FOR ADMISSION — With written questions, attorneys can ask either party to the divorce to admit or deny specific facts. An attorney may ask the opposing party to agree that you acquired an asset prior to the marriage or by gift or inheritance, eliminating that asset as part of the marital property in question.

Admissions can limit the cost of hiring expert witnesses or incurring additional attorney fees to make the determination. Not answering brings its own risk, a move a court might consider an automatic admission.

DEPOSITIONS — Often the most confrontational and important tools of discovery, depositions are taken in person, under oath and your spouse may be present. A deposition can uncover the basis for the opposition's case as well as the substance of witness testimony. Any allowable question must be answered and your attorney should be present to protect you against unfair questions. Remember, though, that revealing too much too easily can help your adversary and perhaps make your case more difficult.

Depositions are formal legal proceedings, not conversations. While you must answer truthfully and completely, your attorney should work with you to prevent you from volunteering information that might help the opposition.

A court reporter will note everything said during a deposition to create a written record. Each party to the divorce can read and memorize the transcript, allowing them to limit the possibility of making a contradictory statement when testifying at trial.

Prepare to name every reason you want the divorce. As with interrogatories, you are often asked to name every person who has knowledge of your case and what he or she will testify to at trial. Work with your attorney to prepare, focusing on remembering the critical parts of the case.

A deposition can shed light on the opposition's entire case. Consider a wife who filed a vicious and accusatory pleading alleging wrongdoing by her spouse. Her attorneys filed the pleading, hoping to put the husband on the defensive. Her deposition, though, showed she lacked the facts to back up the claims. The lack of information unearthed in the deposition could put the wife and her attorney on the defensive, and their case might never recover. While a deposition offers a powerful tool, make sure your strategy and goals demand the added expense. A deposition by your attorney, who must prepare for and conduct the session, can cost you several thousand dollars. Before you take this step, make sure a settlement is impossible, and the information you might learn is worthwhile.

A deposition to learn the specifics of a bank account with a few hundred dollars in it might not deserve the expense. But in instances of high-value, contested assets or child custody, a deposition may represent a powerful, necessary tool.

ELECTRONIC EVIDENCE

Some clients take pride in a successful game of "gotcha." E-mail, computer records and other high-tech resources seem to offer great pathways to the goods. Federal laws and state statutes set specific limits on the scope and methods for collecting this information.

Use care if you hope to collect proof of your spouse's infidelity or gain favorable evidence by reading e-mails, wiretapping the home telephone, eavesdropping on cellular phones, or retrieving records from Internet conversations in chat rooms.

In Georgia, recording a one-on-one telephone conversation is allowed without telling the person on the other end of the call. You cannot, however, record calls involving more than one other person. Also, it is illegal to record calls either to or from a location outside Georgia. If you hope to record your spouse calling an out-of-state romance on a home line, don't expect the court to admit this evidence.

Similarly, Georgia has specific laws preventing someone from creating a false online identity. If you suspect your spouse of seeking new relationships in an online chat-room, for example, this law would prohibit you from entering the chat-room, posing as someone else and attempting to solicit damning admissions from your spouse.

Also, just because you have a computer in the home doesn't mean everyone has access to all of the information. If your computer is protected with a password, your spouse cannot legally gain access to the stored data.

The legality of all these issues, as well as many others involving electronic communication, is complicated and must be approached with care. Your attorney should understand the state and federal laws protecting you and know when and how to legally seek vital information.

10

Financial Planning

Consulting a financial planner can prove one of the most productive steps for a divorcing person. A good advisor can help reduce the tax consequences from divorce settlements, help minimize budget expenses, develop income options and plan major financial decisions. Your attorney or friends you trust can often provide referrals to reputable financial planners.

Andy Berg is co-founder of Homrich & Berg, Inc., in Atlanta. The wealth management company serves 350 clients in 29 states and manages more than $1 billion in investment capital.

Berg said the company often counsels the non-working spouse, helping that person to balance lifestyle choices with the reality of post-divorce finances. Sometimes they help a client chart a course that resembles retirement planning, a future dependent on existing investments and assets. At other times, such as when both spouses work and have ongoing sources of income, a financial planner must help the individual plan to manage a household on less than the joint incomes of a two-earner marriage.

FINANCIAL PLANNING SUGGESTIONS
FOR SECURITY AFTER THE DIVORCE

Whether our clients are high-net-worth individuals or people of average means, we often suggest that they work with financial planners to ease the transition from married to single life. Financial planner Donna Barwick of the Atlanta office of Mellon Financial offers the following 15 suggestions for reaching financial stability during and after a divorce:

1. Make sure you know the true total of your necessary living expenses. Determining this is especially problematic if you have not been paying the bills for your family. Make a budget so that you know what you will need to maintain an acceptable lifestyle after the divorce.

2. Before filing for divorce, try to increase your emergency funds as much as possible. Excess liquidity can only help.

3. Be prepared to pay for the best financial, legal and accounting advice. Don't be turned off because a professional has a high hourly rate, if the advice you get is worthwhile. Faulty advice costs more in the long run. Make sure the advisor's interests are aligned with yours.

4. Be reasonable in your pursuit of luxuries, setting proper limits. After divorce, some people with extra money go a little crazy, taking exotic vacations and buying fancy cars.

5. People in the midst of divorce sometimes get preoccupied and forget to pay their bills on time. Repair your credit if it has

been damaged and check your credit often if you think your ex may have done something to harm it.

6. Seek out financial planning advice before negotiating a final settlement. You probably need expert help to determine how the settlement will affect your future plans. Projections should focus on income and expenses, retirement and insurance needs. In your settlement, push for liquid assets or those with low tax liabilities. Settlements that appear 50-50 may not be equal because of high tax consequences.

7. Factor in your long-term healthcare needs. If you are fairly young and in good health, long-term care insurance is relatively inexpensive. If you are 50 years old or older, look into a policy.

8. If you have special-needs children who will be disabled in their adult lives, requiring your continued care, address their care in the settlement. If they are not eligible for Medicaid, potential expenses should be taken into consideration in the settlement agreement.

9. Try to determine either the amount or percent of college costs each parent will pay when the time comes. There are several tax-advantaged ways to save for tuition expenses.

10. If you are scheduled to receive spousal support or child support over time, make sure these payments are secured by setting up an alimony or support trust or purchasing life insurance on the payor spouse.

11. If you stand to inherit assets, work with your parents to structure those assets in a way, such as a purely discretionary trust, that makes it harder for your spouse to claim them in a divorce action. An inheritance is separate property that cannot

be equitably divided, although one could make an alimony claim, and an inheritance is relevant to the cases.

12. Consider your own estate planning situation. Update your will, perhaps removing your ex-spouse from it and changing beneficiaries on life insurance policies, IRAs, other retirement plans and benefits through your employer.

13. For married people, there is almost never estate tax due at the death of the first spouse because Federal tax laws allow for a marital deduction. After a divorce, with no surviving spouse, there may be liquidity issues that should be addressed and perhaps life insurance can solve the problem.

14. Learn to make your own money decisions with the help of a financial planner. If your former spouse made these decisions for you in the past, you will have to take on this task.

15. Don't make any major financial decisions that you don't have to for at least one year following the divorce. It takes time to adjust to the financial realities of life after divorce.

11

Other Professionals Your Attorney May Enlist

You should choose an excellent attorney to help with your divorce, but understand the case may require the expertise of other specialists. In cases of substance abuse or other criminal behavior, a criminal lawyer might help. A tax attorney might assist with a strategy to divide a business. You might need a corporate transactional lawyer to validate or draft documents, an estate planning lawyer or an expert in bankruptcy law. Besides legal professionals, you may need the help of others.

ADDITIONAL LEGAL SPECIALISTS

You've already hired one specialist, a family attorney steeped in divorce law. While family law attorneys must have knowledge and abilities spanning many areas of the law, they may sometimes draw on specific skills of colleagues. With most family law attorneys working alone or in small firms, it's common for them to seek outside assistance.

Your attorney, for example, might seek the help of a bankruptcy specialist to evaluate if filing for bankruptcy can help your case. This attorney could also evaluate the effects of a bankruptcy by the other side. Such a dramatic step has the potential for lasting financial repercussions, and it deserves an expert opinion.

Only the most complicated cases require an entire team. This may seem like overkill, as if a swarming of professionals might be sucking up hourly fees. But when large assets are involved, your investment in professional advice should save you money. Your attorney should operate as the head of the team, using advice from one or more of the other attorneys to craft a cohesive strategy.

ACCOUNTANTS

During divorce settlement negotiations, you have many options for preparing and filing tax returns. An accountant can accurately estimate the tax consequences of the various decisions and prove invaluable in financially volatile situations or when taxes are a critical part of an agreement.

"You've got to make sure that the division of assets makes sense from a tax standpoint," says David Bokman, president of Asset Management Advisors in Atlanta. "A very important thing to realize is that if there's $100,000 of financial assets, and one spouse gets $50,000 in cash and the other spouse gets $50,000 of appreciated stocks that were bought a long time ago and have a lot of capital gains tax, that's not a fair trade."

Accountants might also dissect a budget, determining the associated personal expenditures. The accountant can use your home or family financial records to create a snapshot of your family's average spending. If one spouse claims to earn less income than the budget allows and has done that over time, this report will show something is amiss. One person might fudge about expenses or have a source of unreported income. An accountant can determine this from a detailed analysis of income and expenses.

Accountants can also evaluate or audit business financial records to determine if a company provides benefits or other perks beyond reported income. Often bank records or other financial documents are used to make these determinations. This type of audit can show if a spouse receives reimbursements, bonuses or commissions not reported as income. Accounting for this income can make a dramatic difference in division of assets and child support.

A closely held business often presents a challenge. Determining the value of the business must include an adjustment to gauge the amount of compensation paid to an employee-owner who owns 100% of the company. The owner may take all money beyond expenses as compensation rather than declaring a business profit. An accountant working as a valuation expert must use a complex calculation to determine the business' true worth based on profit and not simply the owner's income. This process is often contested.

BUSINESS VALUATION EXPERTS

Divorcing couples with a privately held business interest often hire valuation experts to determine a company's worth, an essential part of the division of assets during mitigation or trial. This measure is drastically different from defining the worth of a publicly traded company, which must complete detailed daily, monthly and quarterly financial statements.

With a business owned by one individual, it's much more of a challenge, says Lyn Reagan, a valuation appraiser with Bennett-Thrasher PC in Atlanta. Small businesses rely on tax returns, often not compiling financial records until required by the Internal Revenue Service.

"Small businesses make all of those adjustments at year's end," Reagan says. "If you're trying to determine a valuation in November, you've often only got 11 months of fuzzy data."

Also, it's common for personal expenses, everything from mortgage payments to private school tuition, to be paid from business accounts, Reagan says. In one instance, a business owner bought a Hummer SUV and a Porsche with money from a company account, claiming them as business expenses. While these actions were not illegal, the purchases raised questions about the value of the business.

When valuing a business, the valuation expert must consider the actual worth as well as personal gains. For example, the process might find that a business is worth $100,000 but that there was an additional $10,000 in personal expenses paid from business accounts, Reagan says. The personal expenditures, essentially profit reported as an expense, would be calculated into the business's overall value, raising it to $110,000, Reagan says.

Generally, if several partners are involved in a business, there is greater accountability and less room for one person to control financial statements and bank accounts. The financial picture is often sharper.

Valuations also consider the concept of personal goodwill as opposed to company goodwill. For example, a doctor with a unique expertise and valuable skills provides a personal value, or goodwill, to a business. A valuation expert can determine how much this personal cachet is worth to a business's bottom line, and Georgia courts do not divide the value of this personal goodwill during divorce.

The company goodwill includes items such as property, computer equipment, company cars or other assets, and the value of these assets can be considered as part of an equitable division of property.

A valuation expert's findings and experience often prove invaluable, particularly if a case goes to court. The expert can follow the steps below to help a divorcing person and his or her attorney determine a company's value:

- Gather documents and other information.
- Analyze the situation.
- Apply generally accepted valuation methodologies.
- Consider valuation issues unique to divorce law.
- Issue a report with a value and its rationale.
- Assist in mediation.
- Be available for depositions.
- Testify in court as an expert witness.
- Work with an attorney to devise a creative settlement.
- Work with an attorney to draft deposition and cross-examination questions.

A good valuation expert does not necessarily put your best interest above all else. The evaluator should defend and support the results of the valuation process, which should be a fact-based result rather than a bargaining tool, Reagan says. If the valuation from your expert varies wildly from that of the opposition, a judge or mediator should not simply attempt to average the two amounts. Instead, the goal should be to determine which valuation is correct. Otherwise, valuators would simply artificially inflate the worth of business, and then help negotiate an amount.

ESTATE PLANNERS

No one enjoys planning for death. Divorce, though, does demand a pragmatic approach to estate planning, and people often change their will in anticipation of divorce.

"The best practice is to rewrite the will completely after the divorce is final, omitting any provision for the former spouse," says John A. Wallace, an attorney and estate planner for King & Spalding in Atlanta.

The transfer of assets between spouses in a divorce is usually done without creating tax liabilities. "From that point on, whatever you have in your estate, then you'd better figure out what the tax consequences are if you die and deal with that in your will or something like an irrevocable trust," Wallace says.

More complex is the division of such assets as family businesses, retirement benefits and family limited partnerships. A good estate planner can provide a map guiding you down the safest path through the various tax issues. The planner can also help remove you from potentially awkward long-term agreements that may not be in your best interest.

"With interest in family businesses, family farms or other long-term assets involving one side or the other, normally you try to keep those with the spouse who was the member of that family and make up the difference in other, non-family-type assets," Wallace says. "Often, the non-family divorcee wants them that way as well, because they don't want to be tied into a family that they once were a part of in a marriage and now are not. That's not very comfortable, particularly in any kind of business context."

Also, an estate planner can take advantage of opportunities to minimize estate and income taxes and control the management and ultimate disposition of assets. It's important to change beneficiary designations for employer-sponsored plans including group-term life insurance, 401(k) plans, profit sharing plans or pension plans. These changes usually must be completed on company forms and submitted to the employer to properly go into effect.

While a judgment in a divorce ends the marriage, the work can continue beyond the moment a judge grants the divorce. "A will, of course, can be changed anytime, provided you remember to do it," Wallace says. "So often, after a divorce, the first thing that's done is the client goes and gets a new will, because everything needs to be rethought."

101

APPRAISERS

Fail to agree on the value of an asset? An appraiser can often solve disagreements, or at least provide a foundation for negotiations. These experts are usually hired when a divorcing couple divides assets or when assets are sold and the proceeds divided.

Often a home creates the greatest tension, with each spouse hoping for an estimate that provides the greatest leverage during negotiations. A person hoping to keep the home may tend to underestimate the value, while the person giving up the home might argue for a higher value.

"The appraisal should accurately and effectively communicate the valuation issues to the user of the report so that he or she can react to that information, understand that information," says Dillon H. Fries, an appraiser with Dillon H. Fries & Associates in Atlanta.

Fries recommends that you carefully select an appraiser under the following criteria:

- Ask your attorney for referral to a trustworthy professional appraiser.
- Experience counts. Ask about an appraiser's experience. How often does the appraiser work for divorcing clients?
- Consider an appraiser who also specializes in relocation work. Companies remove poor performers from their list of approved appraisers.
- Is the appraiser willing and able to provide testimony in court?
- Tell the appraiser if the results will be used in divorce proceedings for the division of assets.
- Ask if the appraiser follows the Uniform Standards of Professional Appraisal Practice.
- Does he use a form that provides the proper depth of analysis?

- An appraiser should offer complete, accurate and fair results.

MENTAL HEALTH PROFESSIONALS

Counselors and therapists often address the emotional toll of divorce, but realize that financial strain can create significant stress. Everyone in the family, from the beginning, should understand the ramifications.

Some counselors advise couples to explain shifting financial circumstances to their children, who often become willing participants capable of helping. Children need to understand what is happening, and they do their best when they have information. They need to be told everyone will have to work together to live on what they have.

A child often looks to the parent for cues on coping with divorce and the subsequent financial strain, although the age of the child can shape the reactions, says Dr. Don Bower, head of the the University of Georgia's department of Child & Family Development. "Younger children have almost a sixth sense that picks up on when a parent is stressed," he says. "Children look to their parents to understand if this is something they should be worried about, or if it's routine."

Often children in the age range between pre-school and second grade perceive family problems as their fault, and a parent should provide reassurances. Older children focus on the meaning to the family and themselves. Children who have reached puberty tend to think more about how a divorce and tight finances will change their daily lives, Bower says.

12

Couples Without the Benefit of Marriage

Not all committed relationships lead to marriage. Many couples who are sexual partners choose to bypass marriage but continue to intertwine their personal and financial lives. During the U.S. Census and other population counts, these couples can choose to identify themselves as unmarried partners.

Census 2000 counted 5.5 million couples who described themselves as living together as unmarried partners, up from about 3.2 million in 1990. Differences in the data make direct comparisons difficult. The National Marriage Project at Rutgers University indicates that about a quarter of unmarried women age 25 to 39 currently live with a partner and almost half lived at some time with an unmarried partner. More than half of all first marriages are now preceded by cohabitation, compared to virtually none earlier in the 20th century.

In Georgia, there were about 145,743 unmarried partner households recorded during Census 2000. About 126,455 unmarried couples were opposite sex and 19,288 were same sex.

While living together may not begin with marriage, ending the relationship can bear the same weight that divorce does for a married couple. What happens when the person paying one-half or more of the household expenses decides to leave? What happens with shared purchases of homes or automobiles?

COMMON LAW OR JUST UNMARRIED?

Until 1997, a couple living together in Georgia and essentially acting in all ways as if they were married could claim a common law marriage. The legal change did not invalidate existing common law marriages and ending any such unions does require a divorce. Failing to legally end the marriage and then marrying someone else could result in a bigamy charge.

Now, couples living together have few defined legal rights. Essentially, lawmakers decided that people "living in sin" should not enjoy the same status as married couples. There is no legal right for a court to allow property division or alimony, for example.

When these couples split, they may land in court with a judge trying to untangle the various ownership issues, but there are strategies to avoid such conflicts. An unmarried couple buying property, for example, should consider a detailed property agreement specifying ownership. Similarly, if one person agrees to pay the debts of the other, a contract explaining the transaction can clear up any confusion about the agreement.

CHILDREN OF THE UNWED

The National Marriage Project estimates that nearly half of all children in this country spend some time in a cohabiting family before age 16. The results for unmarried couples with children often include more than complicated living arrangements. If a split occurs, there is no easy way to untangle child custody issues. An existing contract might settle a dispute over a home or a car, but a judge must consider only the best interest of the child when deciding where the child will live.

The decisions can have long-lasting results for these children. Before they reach age 16, three quarters of children born to co-habitating parents see their parents split up, while only about one-third of children born to married parents experience a breakup.

On average, these children display significantly more behavior problems and have lower academic and work performance records than children in intact families. The level of difference depends on the amount of conflict between the parents. Children of unwed parents are more likely to be the subject of child custody battles, conflicts over visitation and child support enforcement fights.

PROVING PATERNITY NOW EASIER

Children born into unmarried unions receive far less child support than children of conventional marriages, according to several studies. Proving paternity is often essential to establishing rights of inheritance and rights to Social Security benefits.

Some fathers refuse to accept these children as their own. Courts widely accept genetic test results to establish paternity. Genetic, or DNA testing, is quick, inexpensive, and accurate. A small blood sample or a simple swab inside the cheek can be used to prove paternity with 99.9% accuracy.

Paternity can have serious financial implications for the two adults and the child. A lifetime of child support for one child can total several hundred thousand dollars for a middle-class family. When a parent dies, Social Security survivor benefits and private insurance can mean the difference between subsistence living and a comfortable life for a child born out of wedlock.

Part Two

Dividing Assets at Divorce

S N A P S H O T

IT'S HER SEPARATE PROPERTY

Her View

Her family had owned the land for generations. As a child, she spent most weekends working the farm and helping her grandparents maintain the farmhouse. It was her heritage. Before the marriage, her grandparents died and she inherited the place.

After the wedding, she and her husband spent many weekends at the farm and he finally suggested making it their home. She loved the idea.

The farmhouse, though, needed significant repairs. He promised to tackle the work on his own but she knew it was a big job and he often lost focus. When she told her parents of the plans, they offered to pay for the restoration. Consider it a gift, they said.

She thought they were so generous. He thought they were meddling again in their married lives. But she couldn't say no and he didn't really like that kind of work. And so the restoration began.

In the early stages of the construction, they fought constantly about the involvement of her parents, who wanted to participate in every decision. They were paying after all. The restoration was taking twice as long as anticipated and tensions heightened with each passing month. And their problem wasn't just the farm. They couldn't agree on anything. She knew she'd been spoiled as a child, but he was a handful. She sought advice from her minister and friends. Could these disagreements really harm their marriage?

She suggested couples therapy. He came to a few sessions, but as soon as the topic turned to the farmhouse, he walked out. She struggled to understand why he couldn't let go of his anger. Shortly after the failed therapy sessions, he moved out.

She contacted a lawyer and filed for divorce. Her lawyer asked her to list their marital property and her separate property.

On her separate property list, she included the farmhouse and surrounding land. It was an inheritance and it would remain in her family.

His View

Since the day they married, he felt he worked to maintain the farm and the farmhouse. He put in countless hours repairing what broke or fell into disrepair, maintaining and even adding to the value of the property. He knew she overlooked the little things they did as a couple to maintain the place, but he remembered.

After spending almost every weekend traveling back and forth to the property, he suggested the move. They enjoyed the laid-back country life but the rundown farmhouse was always a stumbling block.

He planned on doing most of the repairs himself. There were only a few things he couldn't do, and he could oversee the project. He wanted the satisfaction of bringing the farm back to life. That was before she told her parents.

Paying for the renovations was generous, but her parents were so indecisive and cautious. They made the process much more difficult than necessary. Her parents would not allow him to complete any of the repairs on his own. He knew they were spending way too much money on the contractors, but nobody listened.

They argued each day over the progress. Everyone blamed him, but he felt any progress was due to his attention. He didn't hide his frustration when she stuck up for her parents. He no longer saw this as a gift, but a hindrance.

He tried to avoid conversation about the farm. He hated confrontations. Especially when nothing ever got solved. If she could not see his point of view, he just wouldn't talk about it.

He was surprised when she suggested a marriage counselor.

Sure, they weren't communicating well, but only about the farmhouse. Everything else was fine. He agreed to the sessions and hoped the therapist could referee a civilized discussion. But even with the therapist's help, she still refused to consider the meddling of her parents. How could she be so blind?

After these fruitless therapy sessions, he wasn't surprised when she filed for divorce. His attorney asked him to draw up an assets inventory list and indicate the property that was separate and what was marital. For him, the farmhouse was marital. Throughout their marriage, he had spent plenty of his time and effort maintaining the place. He was ready to fight for what was rightfully his.

The Result

Listening to their attorneys, the couple quickly learned that any property acquired during marriage was considered marital and could be divided by the court. Any property, whether land, income or other assets, acquired before marriage remained separate. His attorney said a judge would likely consider the farm her property since it was acquired through inheritance (inherited property even attained during marriage remains separate) and was in her possession before the marriage. For her, the news came as a welcome relief. He was just angry.

In Georgia, though, a judge can make fine distinctions to create an equitable division of property and not just a split of assets. Simply, the court can decide what's fair unless the couple reaches an agreement on their own. And once their case landed before a judge, that's exactly what happened.

The couple attempted to reach an agreement through mediation but tempers and trust frayed. They eventually ended up in court and before a judge, who ruled that the farm remained hers. The judge, though, also acknowledged the sweat equity the husband put into the farm, ruling the work raised the value of the property but not by nearly as much as he wanted. When dividing the remainder of the couple's property, including a boat, two cars and various other assets, the judge said he considered the husband's sweat equity. Neither former spouse was happy with the split, but the court considered it equitable.

13

Making the Most of
Your Assets

A home. Cars. Retirement benefits. A business. Antiques purchased on a fall road trip through the mountains. When a marriage ends, the settlement should detail the fate of everything of value. This property—not just land but all assets of a marriage—faces division.

And for you, there's an essential distinction: equitable versus equal. An equal split would send each person away from the marriage with half the assets. Georgia family law does not work this way. Instead, Georgia provides for an equitable division, which allows the court to distribute property in a manner deemed fair, under the circumstances, but not necessarily equal.

Understanding equitable division demystifies the debate associated with divorce. For Georgia, a case concluding before the state Supreme Court in 1980 established the ground rules.

The case, *Stokes* v. *Stokes*, started simply enough but developed into a precedent-setting action. Through a series of hearings, decisions and appeals over assets such as a family house in Lawrenceville, the case allowed the court to address the property of a married couple.

The court decided a judge or jury should divide marital property, (any property acquired during marriage) equitably between the husband and wife. However, each person could keep any property owned before marriage, no matter whose name was listed as the owner of the property during the marriage.

Also, the courts defined non-marital property, which is not subject to division. For example, any property received as a gift or as inheritance remains separate.

In the end, the Stokes case generated guidelines now generally followed in dividing property in divorce or separation cases and detailed the factors for considering the division.

While each state court system establishes its own rules for dividing marital property, Georgia's approach is common. Forty-one states rely on an equitable division of assets, according to The Equity in Marriage Institute, while the remaining nine states operate under community property rules.

IDENTIFY YOUR ASSETS

Reaching a successful division of marital property begins with a simple step. Identify all assets. Often, creating an inventory is straight-forward. In complex circumstances such as a closely-held business or if one spouse tries to obscure holdings, however, the complexity can prove difficult to unravel.

At first, don't worry if something is marital property. You might have a house, two cars, some rental properties, a 401(k), household items, furniture and jewelry. Just concern yourself with understanding your assets and their location. A review of bank account records, county tax rolls and credit card statements can produce clues to any hidden property.

Marital property can consist of an array of assets eligible for division. Also, a tally must consider any debts or other liabilities associated with individual assets. The property to consider includes the following:

- Artwork
- Antiques
- Automobiles
- Bank and brokerage accounts
- Boats and trailers
- Business interests
- China, silver, crystal
- Collectibles
- Guns and sporting goods
- Home furnishings
- Life insurance and annuities
- Retirement plans (401(k), pension plans and IRAs)
- Stock options, deferred income and bonuses
- Stocks and bonds
- Tools and yard equipment

MARITAL PROPERTY OR SEPARATE PROPERTY?

The essential art of asset division is determining if an asset is marital property or separate property. The court can only divide marital property. Income on property owned separately remains separate.

Income earned during a marriage, however, is considered marital property and can be divided unless the spouses agreed to a prenuptial or postnuptial agreement. In Chapter 27, we discuss these agreements in greater detail. Consider a woman who enters the marriage with $50,000 in a brokerage account.

The original amount remains separate property and the interest or dividends earned on this account during the marriage are probably nonmarital assets as well, depending on whether either of the spouses actively managed the money during the marriage.

Often, though, it's difficult to separate funds mixed and mingled throughout a marriage. Say the wife owned a home outright before marriage. Then, once married, the couple remodels, adding a bedroom, bath and a garage apartment. They use a home improvement loan to pay for these additions, repaying that loan with joint earnings. The couple never agreed to characterize the property otherwise, leaving it as the wife's separate property.

Then, the couple decides to purchase another home and make payments on a mortgage loan by renting the first house. The new home and the income they receive from the rental constitute a mix of marital and separate property, and a portion of the original investment in the home might also represent divisible marital assets.

Unraveling complex threads require outside help. Charles Mittelstadt is president of The Mittelstadt Firm, a division of International Security Consultants, Inc. The company works in investigation and sometimes arranges the services of forensic accountants who can unearth fine details of financial histories.

Services such as Mittelstadt's prove especially helpful when two people disagree over the amount of money that should be available, whether tied to the home or to other accounts. "You can follow the money and establish that it was there at one point in time, even though it's no longer there," Mittelstadt said. "Whichever party might have moved the money will have to provide some explanation, whether it be at trial or through some deposition."

Separate property commingled with marital property generally is considered separate property as long as its source and identity can be traced and it can be easily divided. Where separate and marital property become commingled and defy characterization, the entire asset may be considered marital property.

If significant questions remain, consider seeking the advice of a forensic accountant.

WHAT IS YOUR PROPERTY WORTH?

Assign a value to each piece of property before dividing it. You should expect to provide convincing evidence regarding an asset's value and be prepared to support those values in court. Try to save time and expense by reaching an agreement on values of as many assets as possible.

While difficult to attach values with mathematical accuracy, facts, common sense and informed judgment guide a competent appraisal. The fact-finder, either a judge or jury, determines the value after hearing all the evidence.

And, various types of evidence can define an asset's value.

Each party to the divorce can hire expert witnesses to value their property, and a judge or jury might decide to accept one valuation, discounting the testimony of one expert in favor of the other. In some cases, though, the judge will set a value somewhere between the two estimates.

Owners can even testify about the value of real property if they know the property's market value. People who closely follow the real estate market in their neighborhood might testify to the value of a home. While those testifying may not qualify as experts, if they can show a foundation for their knowledge, their testimony may be worthwhile.

Gauging value requires more than testimony. Documents such as mortgage instruments, sales and earnest money contracts, receipts and bills of sale can all help to define and establish value. Also, market quotations, tabulations, lists, directories or other published compilations can support a value on items ranging from stocks, crops and motor vehicles to antiques, livestock and pedigreed pets.

The Property Division

After identifying, characterizing and valuing marital property, you might expect an easy time with property division. Generally you would be wrong. Property division is often the most difficult part of settlement.

Pride, ego and the need for revenge often cause mature people to trade reason for petty attacks. They may even fight over property unused during marriage. If you don't want the judge telling you whether you get to watch the flat screen television or play with the Xbox, convince your soon-to-be ex to divide the assets with you.

Letting the Court Decide

Some couples, even after determined good-faith attempts, cannot agree on the division of property. And, not all couples even try diligently to reach an agreement. In such circumstances, a judge or jury must make the call.

Remember, though, this approach takes control out of your hands and places the power with a judge or jury, with broad discretion to determine the division of property.

The court will weigh everything, from alimony and retirement benefits to business income and savings. Before committing to going to court, make sure you understand the power you relinquish and the potential risks.

Dividing Assets in a "Just and Right" Manner

In Georgia, the Stokes case helped to establish guidelines for the division of property and the factors a judge or jury should consider when determining what constitutes an equitable split. Those are as follows:

- The length of marriage and any earlier marriage.
- The age, health, occupation, vocational skills and employability of each spouse.
- The services contributed by each spouse to the family.
- The amount and sources of income, property, debts, liabilities and needs of each person.
- Debts against the property.
- Whether alimony will be awarded.
- The opportunity of each spouse to earn money or acquire property in the future.

The court may award a money judgment in favor of one spouse as a means of dividing the marital property. This solution may help a spouse recoup the value of assets lost through the other spouse's actions. If one spouse receives a particularly valuable asset, such as the family home or a business interest, the court may make an equalizing award of cash to the other spouse. Remember, Georgia judges and juries are not required to create an equal split.

A judge and jury wield great discretionary power over such decisions. If you're not willing to risk letting the court decide the fate of your property, consider working harder with your spouse to reach an agreement before going to court.

12 Steps to a More Productive Divorce

No matter whether you are married or just living together, the following steps are essential to emerging from a breakup financially and emotionally intact.

1. Establish goals. Write them down and remind yourself throughout the divorce, and always refer to this list when considering any action.

2. Organize and collect financial information. Establish online access to financial data so you can check balances quickly for any withdrawals. Run a credit report on yourself. This report lists all accounts, account numbers and balances of accounts open in your name.

3. Complete a property inventory. Define each asset and its value. Also, provide the most recent statement for every account listed in the inventory.

4. Choose your battles. Do a cost/benefit analysis. Which assets are important? What are they worth? Are there assets you don't need? Never spend more money fighting for an asset than it is worth.

5. Divide your assets yourself. Try to work with your spouse and decide who gets which assets between you.

6. Be realistic about your ability to retain assets. Don't accept the marital residence unless you know you can pay

for it. If both spouses work and still struggle to pay bills, chances are you can't handle them by yourself.

7. Look for resolution, not revenge. Remaining level-headed will allow you to negotiate a settlement faster. Take mediation seriously. It can save thousands.

8. Consider taxes. What looks good on paper can cost you in the long run.

9. Dote on details. Stay on top of your divorce decree and make sure your spouse is following through on his or her obligations. Do not allow too much time to pass before contacting your attorney regarding an enforcement action.

10. If your spouse concedes a point, reciprocate the favor. Working with your attorney and the other side can settle your case faster than resolving the issue in court.

11. Negotiate for the future. Think in terms of the divorce and potential future litigation when considering a settlement agreement. Current litigation can cost a fraction of what you will spend to go back to court and modify an agreement.

12. Try to remember that you are the mature one in the divorce, working on goals for yourself and your children rather than seeking revenge. Instead of dwelling on the past, move forward with your life.

14

Dealing with the Family Home at Divorce

The family home usually represents the emotional and psychological center of family life. It's more than shelter, greater than a simple asset, and often prized by each spouse. But, in divorce many couples fight over the home only to come to the realization that neither individually can afford to keep it.

The fate of a residence often hinges on who can afford to pay for it after the marital assets are divided, debts are paid and child support is agreed upon.

You may want the home, possibly even feel you deserve it, but you should rely on your attorney or financial advisor to examine your ability to maintain the residence before fighting for it. Learn early if you cannot afford the home, a tough but often essential necessity. After all, why spend time formulating a strategy to acquire an asset you can't afford.

The house becomes an issue the moment you or your spouse file for divorce. In most cases, the party with temporary custody of the children maintains temporary possession of the home because it is the children's residence.

Don't focus on the temporary, though. You eventually must decide how to deal with this most prized asset.

EXAMPLE: Your home may be your most valuable asset

With a large asset such as a home, a property division can create complex awards. Consider this example. You agree to sell the home and come out with $150,000 after paying off the mortgage and deducting the costs of sale. So, each person receives $75,000. Right? Well, maybe, but not always.

Say you also have two automobiles and some household furnishings. Add these together with a 401(k) and you have a value of $50,000 after payment of any loans on any of these items. The marital estate is worth $200,000, but because of several factors the court decides to give your spouse 60% of the assets, or $120,000, and you get 40%, or $80,000. To accommodate that split, one spouse may receive $100,000 in cash from the sale of the home, one fully paid off automobile worth $15,000 and some household furnishings. The spouse who gets 40% of the assets receives the remaining $50,000 from the home sale, an automobile worth $5,000, the remaining furnishings worth $10,000 and the 401(k) worth $15,000.

SELL THE HOME AND DIVIDE THE EQUITY

Putting the home on the market is a common way to divide this asset, selling it and using the proceeds. Usually, the overall settlement spells out the distribution of the proceeds, often either with the money going to one person or a split based on a negotiated formula.

Agreement on a sales price, though, can prove difficult. Ideally, you try to sell the home for the fair market value defined as the amount a willing buyer would pay to a willing seller.

The court may hear the following types of evidence to help determine the proper fair market value of a property:

MARKET DATA — Evidence of recent comparable sales in the area may determine market value.

TAX VALUE — Because property is to be appraised for tax purposes at fair market value, the taxable value of property may provide evidence of the value.

Consider verifying that value by consulting a realtor, allowing you the possibility of avoiding the cost of an appraisal because most realtors know local market values. Look closely at comparable homes already on the market.

You always have the option of acquiring an independent property appraisal. If two independent appraisals differ wildly, you and your soon-to-be-ex can select a third appraiser to value the home.

Setting the price begins the process, but selling a home includes other considerations. A realtor can guide you on necessary repairs and improvements. The realtor selling the home can usually arrange completion of the work at a reasonable price.

Rely on the settlement agreement to specify details such as who pays the mortgage, taxes, insurance and utilities before the sale of the residence. The agreement should define who provides routine maintenance and upkeep, as well as who pays the cost of heating, cooling, roofing and structural repairs.

The agreement should also require the person who lives in the home to keep it clean and orderly, ready for a visit by would-be buyers. Once again, the realtor can outline a sales strategy to appeal to potential buyers.

DETERMINE NET EQUITY IN YOUR HOME

An agreement should specify how to pay off costs associated with a home, or if any other debts in the marital estate can be deducted from the gross sales price. Those home-related costs are:

- Mortgage payoff
- Brokerage commission and costs associated with the sale
- Reimbursement to one of the parties for repairs or improvements on the home to facilitate the sale
- Unpaid property taxes
- Payment of other debts specified in the settlement agreement

The settlement agreement should define the status of the equity, whether to hold it in escrow or divide it based on a formula specified in the agreement.

TRANSFER INTEREST IN YOUR HOME FROM ONE SPOUSE TO THE OTHER

Sometimes, one spouse agrees to give up more assets than necessary to retain the family home. One spouse might agree to transfer interest in the home to the other spouse, with the person giving up the home usually receiving a larger share of cash, retirement accounts, household items or a family business. Relinquishing home ownership may prove wise. A home may not have as much value as one spouse expects or market conditions may prevent a quick sale. Both parties should understand the benefits and risks of this type of decision.

An agreement should also specify the execution of necessary warranty or quit-claim deeds to transfer interest and clarify responsibility for mortgage debt as well as taxes and other expenses.

127

Transfer of an asset to your ex-spouse does not absolve you of
responsibility for the debt unless your spouse refinances the loan
or sells the property and pays off the loan.

Failing to pay the debt or creating roadblocks to an agreed
upon property sale can bring serious repercussions. Breaking
or bending the signed agreement specifying dispensation of the
property can lead a judge to issue a contempt of court citation.
And remember, a judge has no interest in settling disputes over
a home sale.

One hedge against a delayed sell is a settlement agreement defining the brokerage process. For example, a brokerage agreement might require reduction of the price of the home if it remains on the market after six months, with the percentage of the
price decrease clearly stated.

Consider carefully just how much you want the home. Make
sure fighting for the family home is financially sound before committing. Consider the value of staying in the home with the existing mortgage against selling the residence to clear up that long-
term obligation.

When comparing household expenses to a monthly apartment
rental, you may find your mortgage payment less than the going rate for a similar-size apartment. Or, you may find the cost
of homeownership far too expensive in comparison to other options, whether renting or choosing a smaller house. Such comparisons early in the process can help determine whether to keep
the home.

Also, take care to make sure the mortgage lender understands
who bears responsibility for paying for the home.

"The mortgage company is not going to release someone from
the mortgage," says John Hydrick of UBS Paine Webber in Atlanta. "They made the loan based on both people being there to
pay for it. My recommendation is to refinance the home in the
name of the party who will live there. Otherwise, it's going to
stay on your credit report. Say the husband stays in the home and

doesn't pay on time. Three years later there's a foreclosure; that foreclosure's going to go on the wife's credit, too."

TEMPORARY USE BY ONE SPOUSE

There is no opportune time for divorce, especially when considering the lives of children. Factor in the need to sell the family home, and emotional and financial considerations often conflict.

A divorce settlement can, however, allow some flexibility. A settlement might allow the parent with primary child custody to occupy the home for a specified time after the divorce. After the agreed date, the home is sold and the equity divided.

For example, say you have one child who is a high school junior and another entering high school in two years. A divorce and subsequent move could mean a hardship for them. To minimize the disruption, the divorce agreement might allow you to stay in the home with the children until the older child graduates. Then you move during the summer, when the younger child begins the transition to a new school and the older child prepares to leave the nest.

The settlement agreement should specify the duration you have use of the residence and the events triggering sale of the home. Spell out who is responsible for the mortgage payment and who provides routine maintenance, upkeep and repairs.

While offering benefits, an agreement to delay the home sale can bring complications, such as division of equity at the point of sale. One spouse paying the mortgage and other costs over two years, for example, creates a complex situation. Most homes appreciate in value over time. The person paying the mortgage and other expenses often wants credit for the increased value.

The settlement agreement should contain an agreed formula for calculating the amount of increase and how it will be apportioned. While complex, such flexible home options can work if specifically and accurately defined.

When a Judge Must Decide

Often divorcing couples fail to agree, putting the fate of a home in the hands of a judge or jury.

A court can impose any of the remedies discussed in this chapter. If the home is a marital asset, the judge may order the sale of the home and decide who receives the equity. Or, one person may receive the home even while the other continues to make mortgage payments. Also, the judge may allow one person to remain in the home for a certain amount of time, after which the home is sold and the equity divided.

Remember all of the factors open to review by a judge or jury. The future ability to earn income. The health of a spouse. The odds for an individual's future employability. Subjective by design, the process of divvying up property gives great power to the court. Make sure you understand the ramifications before ending settlement negotiations.

Consider Your Housing Options

Always evaluate your housing alternatives before deciding what to do with your home. People sometimes give up their home but later realize they can't afford an acceptable replacement in the community where they want to live. This proves especially critical for families with children. After you identify an acceptable price point, answer the key questions:

- What type of housing fits your lifestyle (home, townhouse, apartment)?
- Are those housing types available where you want to live?
- How much does housing cost?
- Is the housing you want in your current school district or a comparable one?

- Do you have enough cash for the down payment, closing costs, possible improvements and the first mortgage payment?
- What type of mortgage is available?

"A home is an investment," says Glennis Beacham, a real estate agent in Atlanta. "When I sell a home, I think about that return on investment. And in doing that, we concentrate on getting the best house for their budget in the best area."

Even though she sells homes for a living, Beacham sometimes counsels divorcing clients to take stock of their situation before buying a home on their own. It's a calculation based on both practicality and emotion.

"If you're living in one neighborhood, which you're used to and your children are used to, and you go through a divorce, and you're faced with moving, you change everything — your set of friends as an adult, and your children's friends and their school. You no longer recognize people at the grocery store. You lose all your roots. And then you're not happy and you're not as productive.

"And you've got to maintain your happiness, or you're not going to get out of this situation you're in. The only way you can become productive is to be stable. And to completely uproot and go to a different neighborhood or location is traumatic on adults and on children, so I don't consider that a feasible option. You stay within your general locale, but you don't live in nearly as nice a place," she says.

Tax Matters Related to a Home

With all of the other considerations of a home sale and a divorce, don't forget the IRS. The tax consequences associated with the transfer or sale of the home to a third party could affect the value of the award. There is no taxable gain or loss when the transfer of property takes place between spouses or former spouses. Homeowners can use the equity in their homes to pay off other bills, often a more prudent choice than cashing in a retirement plan that might have a penalty for early withdrawal or a more heavily taxed account that includes stocks and bonds. In some cases, you can even deduct the interest you pay on a home equity loan from your taxes. Consult a tax expert to consider all possible moves.

"A lot of times you can take the $10,000 worth of credit card debt that you have that you're having to pay $300-400 a month on at 27%, and you're able to move it into a mortgage rate, which is going to be at 5 or 6%," mortgage banker Hydrick says. "You get to write that off on your tax return as well, and it's going to lower the payment for you.

"Say you're refinancing the house you live in, the house is worth $300,000 and you owe $200,000, you can refinance it for $210,000 — you're lowering your interest rate on the other debt. The problem is, a lot of times folks pay the debt off, put it into their mortgage and six months later, the debt is right back on the credit card."

PLAY IT SAFE: DO A TITLE SEARCH

Making assumptions when it comes to the disposition of an asset as large and important as your home can be dangerous. Before signing any agreement on that property, review the loan documents and do a title search to make certain no liens were placed on the property without your knowledge.

Here's one example of how a lapse can generate significant costs. A young mother receives the home in the divorce. She earns just enough to pay the mortgage and upkeep on the home for the first year. One day she receives a notice from her mortgage company that her loan carries an adjustable rate and the payment will nearly double the next month.

Upset with her husband for choosing the adjustable rate loan without explaining the downside to her, she decides to sell the home, take the equity and find something affordable for herself and her children. She lists the home with a realtor and agrees to an offer in two weeks. She gets her asking price and decides to save the proceeds and rent an apartment until she finds the right home.

A week before the closing, her realtor calls to say that a required title search uncovered two liens on the property from judgments recorded against her ex-husband. She has no way to satisfy the judgments, which total more than her equity. At closing, she must sign over all the proceeds from the sale to the creditors. She is left with no money and no way to purchase a replacement home for her family.

Never just assume a home represents a valuable asset. The young woman in our story could have avoided this problem by doing a title search before accepting the home in the division of property.

S N A P S H O T

WHO CAN AFFORD THE FAMILY HOME?

Her View

She dreamed of a house with a big backyard. After they married, she saved every spare dime for a down payment on their first home. They purchased a fixer-upper for a good price, and she was thrilled. He wasn't so sure.

While he described the house as a potential money pit, she hoped he would relax and enjoy their new home once they unpacked. With both of them working, she knew they could swing the mortgage payments. When the twins arrived two years later, she quit her job to care for the children, eliminating one paycheck.

Two young children and a juggling act for a household budget wore on their relationship. They fought about money for repairs on the house. She tried to improve their home environment, and he planned projects he never completed. She usually finished the job.

The tension was unbearable, and she felt every discussion turned into an argument. Tired of even pretending their family was happy, she decided only a separation could unravel their problems.

She filed for divorce six months after they separated, knowing tough times would follow. She just wanted to keep the children and the family home. That would make everything all right.

His View

He felt she nagged him about the house from the moment they said, "I do." He enjoyed the limited responsibilities of a couple with no children, no house and no worries.

He wanted to make her happy, though, so he gave into her desire to own a home. Their savings helped buy a rundown old house needing a lot of work. He knew closing on the house put an end to lazy Saturday afternoons.

While he worked long hours to make ends meet, she was relentless. No matter how many hours he worked, she lined up repair projects for evenings and weekends. He finally confronted her. He refused any other projects. She wanted the house, she could maintain it.

He was even relieved when she suggested separation, because he didn't want the blame for ending the marriage.

The Result

The divorce divided their only asset, the house. They didn't have anything else to split, and there was little equity in the home. She was adamant about keeping the old place, and she refused to move their children to a new neighborhood. Breakup of the marriage was enough stress already for the twins.

He argued they should sell and cut their losses. After all, they both needed money for living expenses and attorney's fees. Even with no spare money between them, she wouldn't relent. The final divorce agreement allowed her to keep the house. While she didn't count on having to reimburse him for half the equity, she willingly paid that price.

After six months of trying to hold things together on her own, she finally sold the family home. She simply could not afford to keep it.

15

Dividing the Family Business

For some marriages, the largest asset often proves the most difficult to divide: a family business. This anecdote gives an idea of the challenges in dividing this asset.

He founded an automobile-service business during the mid-1980s. The business enjoyed tremendous growth even as his marriage deteriorated. Even worse, he failed to predict both his company's success and his divorce's venom.

The man didn't take the most basic precautions to guard his business from a divorce. The business represented most of their assets. He realized he must sell his business to raise the cash necessary to settle the divorce. He received two offers on the company. One offer was for considerably more money paid out over several years. The woman didn't want to trust the buyer's ability to pay out the amount over time, and she forced the man to take the lower, all-cash bid.

WHO GETS THE BUSINESS?

No divorce should require the sale of a closely held business, especially if the business owner engages in basic premarital divorce planning. When the business is owned prior to the marriage, a prenuptial agreement or a partnership agreement among the business owners can eliminate most problems.

If you can prove you owned the business prior to marriage, the earnings from the business during the marriage may or may not be marital assets depending on the efforts of the spouses toward the business during marriage. Most businesses created during the marriage go to the party running the business. By this arrangement, the non-owner spouse might receive other assets to offset the value of the interest given to the business owner, including a cash settlement from money borrowed by the owner spouse or payments over time. Rarely will a judge divide a functioning business between two antagonistic spouses in a way that requires them to cooperate in the running of the company. Some divorced couples choose to inflict such an arrangement upon themselves to keep the business intact.

Other strategies can address children and how a divorce impacts their holdings in a business. You can place your business assets in a family limited partnership to benefit children of a previous marriage. The general partners (the parents, for example) control the business while granting limited partnerships to children. A divorce would not end the limited partnerships, allowing children a clear stake in a company.

"The only caveat is that the IRS may try to attack the tax benefits," Atlanta attorney Bob Holt says. "This is an issue of federal income tax, applying in all states. Before any such entity is created, seek advice from an income tax specialist."

Businesses with multiple owners usually avoid the uncertainty of domestic relations court by instituting shareholder or buy/sell agreements that restrict the transfer of equity ownership.

138

These agreements set the rules for any change of ownership, including those caused by death, disability or bankruptcy, as well as divorce. Most business owners resist the transfer of ownership interest outside of the initial core group of investors. Buy/sell agreements give the original group rights of first refusal to purchase the interest before a transfer to someone such as a divorcing spouse.

VALUING THE BUSINESS

Business owners often manipulate the value of closely held firms, and the court often seeks definitive evidence from business valuation experts.

Few family businesses appear on any stock exchange. With no public stock, you cannot merely add up the value of shares to arrive at the worth of a business. Also, each spouse may approach the task with very different goals.

The spouse who wants to keep the business usually argues for the lowest possible value. A low value might limit the amount of compensation paid to the other divorcing spouse, requiring the business owner to produce less cash.

Businesses can also receive low valuations for very valid reasons. A new product may fail or most of the value may be tied to the owner spouse's personal skills and abilities, an asset known as personal goodwill.

While the spouse hoping to retain the business may seek an expert who values the business as high or as low as possible, an effective evaluator will focus on determining the proper value rather than simply finding a way to support an argument that favors his or her client.

A valuation should include an audit of business records to help determine the company's worth. Also, your attorney should examine tax returns and other corporate documents, including profit and loss statements and records used to secure financing.

In more complex cases, a business appraiser looks at the following information to form an impression of the value:

- The nature and history of the business
- Its tangible assets
- The earning capacity of the business
- Fair market value of all assets
- Amount of goodwill with customers and suppliers

Your lawyer must gain some understanding of the possible ranges of value of the business from the expert to analyze a settlement or assess the likely outcome at trial. Somewhere along the way, you must persuade a judge or jury of the reasonableness of a certain value.

PROTECTING YOUR ASSETS

141

Dental Practice A Major Asset

Her View

Putting him through dental school was one of the toughest challenges of her life. Between studying and completing the required internships, he didn't earn any real money. She kept them afloat financially, and he promised to end their money worries once he completed his degree.

She helped him open their first office shortly after graduation. To keep employee overhead low, she worked three days a week as office manager. They built the practice together, and she thought it was as much her business as it was his. She knew he wasn't crazy about her working close to him, and she thought of this arrangement as temporary.

After six years, the practice flourished and they opened a second clinic on the other side of town. She took pride in the success but also felt she earned some time off.

She directed her efforts into redecorating their Dunwoody home. She hosted lavish cocktail parties, networking with well-connected friends and neighbors. Even though she was not in the office every day, she felt she still worked on behalf of the business.

He attended the parties and mingled with their friends but didn't appear comfortable around that crowd. Ill suited to the art of schmoozing, he would make an appearance and retreat to his study.

She despised that room where he spent most of his time. She begged him to spend more time with her, but he grew more sullen and withdrawn.

One evening, he came home from work and said the stress of managing two offices was too much. He intended to close the second location. She could not remember the last time he talked to her about the practice. She offered to return to her old position, but he dismissed her efforts with a wave of his hand.

She could feel the distance between them growing. She spent more time with her friends while he locked himself away in his study. She pleaded with him to attend marriage counseling, but he refused to talk about their problems. As time passed, she could feel the cracks in their marriage widening.

He surprised her by offering to move into an apartment. Realizing he was certain to file for divorce, she wanted the upper hand. The next morning, she called a divorce attorney recommended by a friend. She told the lawyer she didn't care about the house or the car. She wanted her fair share of their dental practice.

His View

For him, the years of dental school were trying, but he didn't complain. He knew she did a lot for them, but he hated her martyr act.

When he opened the practice, he had no idea what to expect. When she offered to work in the front office, he agreed but worried about how well they would work together. He was pleasantly surprised by her efficiency and never worried about the accounts or insurance claims.

After five years, the practice generated substantial profits, and she lobbied for a second office. His instincts told him to wait a few more years, but she insisted they could double their money. With the accountant on her side, she kept at it until she finally wore him down.

With the opening of the second office, she decided to retire. He thought she would grow restless after a few months and come back to work. He began to think otherwise when she started interviewing office managers to take over her position.

Her retirement hit his wallet hard. It was amazing how much money she could spend in one week. She made things worse by taking shopping trips with her friends to New York and antiquing in New Hampshire.

Their home looked fine, but she began to redecorate. When she finished, it no longer felt comfortable to him.

He could tolerate her spending and redecorating, but he hated her parties. He didn't like her new friends. She would plead with him to attend, constantly harping on him about the importance of networking. He told her she did enough networking for them both.

With the pressure of maintaining two offices, he worked closely with his accountant to improve profits. He wondered how he could provide for her lifestyle. She rarely asked about the practice, and she didn't care as long as the money was there. She wanted the money from his business, but she complained about his constant work. If he didn't work, she couldn't play. Arguments always led to days of silence around the house.

He finally decided to close the second office, and he made up his mind to end the marriage.

When he met his attorney, he said he wanted her to have the house, her car and some cash. He wanted sole ownership of his practice. She helped start it, but it would be nothing without his name and degree.

The Result

You could see the clouds of war erupting over the business. Both sides wanted the same thing. And since they had no children, splitting the practice took the focus of the divorce.

He felt giving up the house should keep her from taking a portion of the practice. How could she think the practice would survive without him? She felt she put as much of herself into the practice as he had. She didn't understand why he should benefit solely from the profits of business in the future.

He knew the current status of his practice. Revenue dropped with the *closing of the second office and the lost time connected to the divorce. His expert placed a value on the practice of $500,000. Only remembering when the two-office practice provided a lavish lifestyle, she valued it at $3.5 million.*

They each brought their attorneys and business valuation experts into court. The judge set a value closer to his valuation. The rationale was that much of the value was the result of his personal goodwill, as opposed to the goodwill generated by other factors (location, good staff, advertising). In Georgia, the personal goodwill of one party is not usually marital property. The judge also threw their other assets into the pot, including the house, both their cars and some retirement accounts.

In the end, she retained the house and her car and he was ordered to pay her half of the assets over time. He kept all rights to the business.

Favored Business Entities

The specific form of the business may affect its value and divisibility in a divorce. The most common forms include:

- Sole Proprietorship
- General Partnership
- Limited Partnership
- C Corporation
- S Corporation
- Limited Liability Company (LLC)

Sole Proprietorships

A sole proprietorship is the simplest business entity, often operated in an informal manner. The individual owner may operate financially out of a personal bank account and physically from a desk in an extra bedroom, while creating real wealth for himself and his family. The sole proprietor receives all the profit from the venture and is personally responsible for all business debts. In addition, the sole owner is personally liable for any damages the business might cause.

Because of its simplicity, the sole proprietorship is the easiest form of business to divide in a divorce—if you can trace the business dealings and substantiate the value. The downside of dealing with a sole proprietorship in a divorce is that many of its business practices are inside the head of the owner.

Such a business created during the marriage from marital funds can usually be divided at divorce. If one spouse begins a business before marriage or with separate funds during marriage, that business may remain separate property of the business owner. Profits created by the business and additional assets acquired by the business are marital property.

General Partnerships

A general partnership can represent a very complex entity formed with two or more individuals, corporations or limited liability companies. Such a partnership is an entity distinct from its partners.

Property of the partnership does not belong individually to the partners, but to the partnership. Even if a married couple comprises a partnership, the court cannot award specific partnership property to either person since the property is owned by the partnership and not the individual.

For instance, two spouses may be the sole partners in a general partnership that owns a fleet of transport trucks. When the couple divorces, the partners cannot simply divide the trucks in a way they consider equitable without first dissolving the partnership. They can only divide their interest in the entity that owns the trucks. If a man is in partnership with several other people and he divorces, the couple may agree to split the partnership interest or the judge may award part of it to the man's wife if this is not prohibited by the partnership agreement. Your attorney can help you divide this interest.

Each partner is generally responsible for income taxes on his or her share of the partnership income. If the partnership has losses, each partner may deduct a pro-rata portion of the loss from his income.

Even though specific rules govern the transfer of partnership interests, the attitude of the other partners can determine how easy it is to make productive use of those interests. If you accept a minority partnership interest in your divorce settlement, the actions of the other partners can affect the value of your interest. The partners may not want to buy out your share or you may get responsibility only for the debts of the business. Look closely at the situation before accepting such an interest as part of the settlement.

Limited Partnerships

This form of partnership is more specialized and structured and includes two categories of partners: a general partner and a limited partner. The general partner has unlimited liability for the debts of the partnership while limited partners usually have no liability beyond the amount of their ownership.

The general partner has expansive management responsibilities. A limited partner usually does not have any management responsibilities or involvement in the day-to-day operation of the business. Because a limited partnership interest is more narrowly written than a general partnership interest, being a limited partner may give a spouse tremendous safety and financial security. But it could also award you a title that carries little or no authority to influence a change or receive any financial benefit from the partnership.

Your attorney should examine the limited partnership documents and determine what interest is transferable under the partnership and if accepting such an interest is a good business decision.

Corporations

A corporation can be a small business with one shareholder or a multinational company with publicly traded stock and thousands of shareholders. The following defines what stock is marital property and what is separate property.

Stock in a corporation incorporated during marriage is typically considered marital property.

Stock acquired before marriage, or during the marriage by gift or inheritance, is separate property. Any increase in the value of corporate stock belonging to a separate estate due to natural growth or the fluctuations of the market remains separate property.

If the increase is due, at least in part, to the time, toil and talent of either or both spouses, the stock remains separate property, but the marital estate may have a right to reimbursement.

Like a partnership, a corporation is a legal entity with an identity separate from its owners. Shareholders of the corporation do not individually own the corporation's assets and generally are not responsible for corporate debts. Following are the two most common types of corporations.

C Corporation — This is the simplest type of corporation. With a C Corporation, the business entity itself owes federal income taxes on earnings. The divorce court has the authority to award a spouse's corporate ownership to the other spouse. If the other shareholders own a majority of the stock and don't want to cooperate with the spouse who received the stock interest, that spouse cannot control ownership of the company. You need to get a clear understanding of the assets and debts of the business, as well as what the corporate documents provide.

S Corporation — This is perhaps the most common form of corporate entity for a closely held business. A sole proprietor may convert his business into an S Corporation for income tax planning and liability purposes. With an S Corporation, the profits and income tax liabilities flow through to each individual stockholder on a pro-rata basis. The corporation itself does not pay federal income taxes.

Examine the corporate documents to see the management of an ownership interest. If you hold a minority interest and the corporation is not publicly traded, that ownership interest could be of little value. But many S Corporations are very successful and a spouse's interest in the business can be worth quite a lot. Even if your spouse doesn't believe the business interest is worth much, other members of the business community may be willing to pay for it. If the corporate documents allow for the transfer or sale of your interest, you could receive tremendous value for it. Analyze the actual value of the corporation to determine if this is an interest worth pursuing.

LIMITED LIABILITY COMPANIES

A limited liability company (LLC) combines elements of a partnership and a corporation. Like a corporation, the liability is limited to a member's individual investment in the entity.

This type of entity is common for professional organizations such as medical practices and law firms. The task of dividing the assets of an LLC at divorce is apparent in these professional types of businesses.

An attorney or a surgeon may own an interest in a limited liability company, but it would be impractical or prohibited for the attorney's spouse to own or control that interest. It is the particular skill of that professional that makes the LLC valuable. Unless the spouse has the same skill, the spouse's interest is worth considerably less under his or her ownership.

It's usually more worthwhile for a spouse to receive other assets or payments over time for part of the ownership interest, rather than attempting to manage a share of the limited liability company.

The same questions that apply to LLCs are relevant to other business entities. What interest in the enterprise can and would you receive? What is that interest worth? Can you sell it now or must you hold it for a time? Can you reasonably and responsibly manage your interest in the enterprise? If the interest is not easily transferable when you need the money, what other assets are available in the marriage to compensate you?

All of these issues should be examined in close detail with your legal counsel to determine options available for ownership of various business interests.

Tax Liabilities of the Business

No matter what form your business takes, each carries tax ramifications. You may have little knowledge of the business or its tax history and the divorce agreement may give your spouse responsibility for tax consequences. Still, the Internal Revenue Service may declare both of you responsible for any liability. If so, you may need to seek relief from the divorce court, increasing the importance of the specific language of the divorce agreement. The agreement should state that the responsible spouse will hold the other harmless for any future problems related to income tax liabilities.

16

Retirement Benefits/
Stock Options

Preparing for retirement demands care. Too many people
have learned the dangers of not preparing. During the
1990s economic boom, an overheated stock market fueled an emphasis on tax-deferred investments, with companies such as En-
ron filling accounts with valuable corporate stock. Thousands of
people lost their life savings when the company crumbled.

And with eroding confidence over the future of Social Security, well-tended 401(k) retirement accounts and other investment tools constitute increasingly important and valued assets.
Consider these critical resources when preparing for divorce. Retirement accounts often represent some of the largest assets in a
marriage. Generally, benefits accruing before marriage remain
the employee's separate property. Benefits accruing during marriage generally become marital property and a judge or jury may
divide these assets.

A court-ordered divorce decree must determine the rights of both spouses to pensions, retirement plans, annuities, individual retirement accounts, employee stock options and similar plans.

In Georgia, though, remember that the courts define retirement benefits acquired during marriage as marital property subject to division, depending on the particular benefits at issue and the facts of the case. The court may consider the actual contributions of the spouse who is not earning the retirement benefits, the number of years of marriage in which contributions were made, and the degree of a spouse's expected reliance on these future funds.

As with all property division issues in Georgia, the court can make a subjective decision. While courts may award each spouse his or her own benefits, a judge or jury faces no requirement to equally divide marital retirement assets. If retirement benefits of one spouse exceed those of the other spouse, the court may compensate by awarding assets such as home equity or available cash to the spouse with the smaller retirement nest egg.

Complicating the equation is the uncertainty of how quickly and how much a benefit may grow. While assets in retirement plans tend to increase over time, most plans hinge on outside variables. Just ask anyone who saw personal retirement accounts tumble during the late 1990s as the technology bubble deflated.

Also, fundamental changes in the nation's retirement system can throw wrinkles into asset division. Pension plans, once the bulwark of personal retirement, increasingly face challenges. Many companies phased out the plans, ending the idea of providing employees checks for life. Struggling companies have even turned their pension plans over to the federal government in greater numbers than ever. Retirees can no longer count on the absolute certainty of their pension continually growing or even being there over time.

The health of an employer, however, isn't the only potential drag on retirement, and the pre-divorce actions of a spouse can cause damage. Before filing for divorce, someone can withdraw significant amounts to reduce a retirement plan's value. In most 401(k) plans, the spouse contributing to the plan does not have to seek the other spouse's permission before withdrawing funds or obtaining a loan. You should analyze the legitimacy of any withdrawn funds.

QUALIFIED DOMESTIC RELATIONS ORDERS (QDRO)

A Qualified Domestic Relations Order divides a retirement plan into separate portions for each spouse under a property settlement agreement or divorce decree. These QDRO orders apply to tax-qualified plans and 403(b) plans but exclude IRAs.

A QDRO allows you to divide a plan and avoid immediate tax consequences. The spouse who did not participate in the plan but who received a portion of the money in divorce pays taxes only when receiving benefits from the plan. Simply, the money is not taxed when divided at the time of the divorce.

The former non-contributing spouse may face provisions of the plan that applied to the original participant. For instance, the participant's birth date may dictate the timing of any distribution to the former spouse, even if the participant is older.

If you plan to use the money immediately, meet with your accountant to determine the account's net value. Also, a spouse not fully vested in the account may never receive all of the money held in the account.

SURVIVOR BENEFITS

Always plan for the inevitable. No one enjoys considering death, but you can't afford to overlook the financial reality.

As many as 22% of divorced female retirees live in poverty, a higher percentage than widows and women who never married, according to federal statistics. And many ex-husbands die without survivor benefits for their former wives.

Divorce law generally remains gender neutral but issues of survivor benefits tend to affect more women, particularly those who never worked out of the home and who intended to depend on their husband's retirement investments. A woman could end up with nothing if her attorney does not give proper weight to these decisions.

A settlement agreement should address if retirement plan survivor benefits are applicable in the event of a spouse's death. If the divorce occurs before a retirement plan's participant retires, the non-participant spouse might receive a separate interest in the participant spouse's benefits. This can work to the non-participant spouse's advantage, because it can mean that once his or her benefits commence, they continue to be paid for the remainder of that spouse's life, even if the participant spouse dies.

If the participant spouse dies before reaching retirement age, benefits for the non-participant spouse can be at risk. This situation requires a QDRO with a pre-retirement survivor annuity. If the participant spouse has already retired and is receiving benefits when the parties divorce, the non-participant spouse could receive a shared interest, where monthly benefits are paid to the non-participant former spouse over the life of the participant. Even if the participant retires and elects a survivor benefit during marriage, the form of benefit cannot be changed as a result of the divorce.

There can be a cost associated with providing a former spouse survivor annuity, particularly under retirement plans maintained by the federal government. For example, if the total monthly pension payment is $1,000, the parties may agree to divide the payment equally. Under this scenario, each party receives a monthly payment of $500 as his or her share of the benefit. If the plan charges $100 per payment for providing a survivor benefit, the total monthly payment is $900 and each party receives $450 per month. Not all retirement plans allow the transfer of benefits, and there are usually specific language requirements that must be met. If this concerns you, consult your attorney and examine what interests are available under the existing retirement plan.

MILITARY RETIREMENT BENEFITS

The inclusion of military retirement benefits as marital property once remained unclear. Now, a non-military spouse can receive an award of these retirement benefits in a divorce.

Determining the marital property portion of these assets often proves especially complicated. Pay special attention to the language in the agreement or decree concerning these benefits. Consult with your attorney to address if the military requires a special type of order, such as a qualifying court order, or other records before payment to the former spouse of a military member.

BORROWING AGAINST YOUR RETIREMENT

Borrowing from a retirement plan, unless you have no other choice, is a bad idea. That makes perfect sense. But if you need cash to settle a divorce, tapping a retirement account is one option. Remember, there are no provisions for borrowing against your IRA (traditional or Roth) or SEP. Borrowing is typically only allowed from a tax-qualified defined contribution plan, such as a 401(k) or 403(b).

Loans from retirement accounts give access to retirement plan money (within limits) without the 10% early distribution penalty for money removed from the plan before age 59 1/2. If repaid according to its terms (normally within five years), money borrowed against a plan is not taxed. Failure to repay the loan triggers the 10% income tax penalty.

It's usually easy to obtain a retirement plan loan, which rarely carries additional expenses. Particularly for people with poor credit, securing a loan from a retirement plan is often easier than receiving one from a commercial lender. And instead of paying interest to a lender, the plan participant pays interest to himself. Most 401(k) plans allow such loans, but check with the benefits department at the company sponsoring the plan before spending the money.

And don't think the IRS won't notice a withdrawal from a retirement plan. When you take money out, you and the IRS receive copies of Form 1099-R from the plan's administrator at the beginning of the following year. Be sure to keep your copy of the 1099-R in your records to verify the exact amount withdrawn.

DIVIDING STOCK OPTIONS

Employer-granted stock options are a popular employee incentive, although interest cooled somewhat after the bust of the dot-com bubble. Still, options can provide substantial assets in case of divorce.

According to the National Center for Employee Ownership, about eight million workers now have option plans, down about two million from just a few years ago.

A stock option gives an employee the right to buy a designated number of shares of the employer's stock within a specified period of time at a certain price. If the company grows and becomes more successful, the value of the stock increases. If the company falters and the stock price goes down below the options price, the options are "underwater" and worth nothing until the stock price rises.

Stock options generally fall into the category of marital property granted and vested during the marriage. Unvested stock options granted during the marriage may or may not be marital assets, depending on why they were granted and what must be done to have them vest. Stock options are often contentious aspects of divorce negotiations. Experts differ on the best way to divvy up options, especially unvested ones.

Turn to a financial planner for advice on the value of stock options versus other assets, although predicting the future worth of stocks is inexact at best. Try to gauge the potential growth as well as the liquidity of each asset before accepting one in a divorce settlement.

S N A P S H O T

The Sometimes Forgotten Assets

His View

For the first 15 years of their marriage, they worked together as a team. She took care of the house, worked part-time and volunteered at their children's school while he earned a good living for their family. He considered their marriage ideal.

He worked hard and loved his career. But he was a low-key guy in a large organization that prized sales acumen. Passivity, he knew, was a problem, so he worked long hours and took on projects his fellow workers would not touch.

She complained long and hard about his work hours. When finally promoted to middle management, she blasted him for all the time he spent away from home. She was incensed that he left little time for family vacations or attending his children's extracurricular activities.

He figured she wanted it all, a fancy lifestyle and a husband who was home when she needed him. One day, he was going through a stack of papers in one of her desk drawers when he found the letter. From its contents, he could tell she was having an affair with another parent from their children's school.

When he confronted her, the tears flowed. He felt angry and guilty at the same time. Angry because she cheated on him, guilty because he shared part of the blame. Maybe he should have listened when she complained about being lonely, but that still didn't give her the right to step out on him.

Within a few days he moved into an apartment. He asked the company lawyer to recommend an attorney. The whole thing was so disturbing that it took another week for him to call that family lawyer. During the initial interview, he told the lawyer about his broken marriage.

He didn't want revenge. He just wanted out without harming his children any more than necessary.

The attorney told him the divorce was fairly simple. As much as 75% of their estate was tied up in his 401(k), and so he would have to share it with her. He was surprised. He never imagined she could take part of his retirement. He was the one who worked to set up the account. She knew nothing about it. She never even asked about their retirement.

The more he thought about his cheating wife taking half of his 401(k), the angrier he got. It was his hard-earned money that contributed to the account. How could she possibly ask for a dime?

Her View

For her, the marriage was fine at first. She focused on the home and the kids while he went to work. But over time, she saw less and less of him. She didn't go looking for the affair. It just happened. Lonely for a long time, she desperately wanted someone to pay attention to her. The children were growing up and didn't need her as much. She felt useless and unwanted and a little bit dead inside.

That's when she started to see another man, who made her feel wanted. She thought she safely hid all of the letters, but she knew the marriage was over when he found one. She called her sister, who recently experienced her own divorce. She gave her the name of an attorney and she set up a meeting. She told the lawyer up front that the breakup was primarily her fault, but years of neglect led her to stray.

The lawyer asked her to list her goals. At the top of the list, she mentioned taking care of their children and making sure she was not penniless. After 15 years of part-time work, she didn't know her chances of finding a decent full-time job.

The lawyer told her to go home and make a detailed inventory of their assets. Later that night, she sat in the study, looking through the drawers of financial records. She paid some of the bills, but he took care of all the other financial matters. She found statements from their bank accounts. Then she found the statements for his 401(k). She didn't remember him talking about opening this account. As she thumbed through the paperwork, she realized this was the family's largest asset. If she could get some of that money, she wouldn't have to worry about finding a job right away.

The Result

Both sides felt partly to blame for the divorce. This allowed them to display the civility necessary to meet face to face in settlement negotiations.

He just wanted the whole mess to end. He worked hard to build up his retirement account and didn't want to see it disappear. He met with his lawyer before their first settlement conference to come up with offers that protected his retirement.

When the time came, he agreed to sell their home and give her the equity, enough money for her to live on for the next several years. She also received most of the home furnishings and their best automobile. When divorcing parties divide a retirement account, the parties enter a Qualified Domestic Relations Order (QDRO) that allows the division and protects the spouse who is a member of the retirement plan from paying taxes on the portion that goes to the non-member spouse.

To satisfy his need to maintain control over the 401(k) account, instead of using a QDRO he offered to pay her quarterly payments equal to her portion of the retirement account.

But his proposal made her an unsecured creditor having to depend largely on his salary to make the payments. Moreover, she would be unable to roll these installment payments over into an IRA or another tax-qualified plan.

Finally, he was persuaded that using a QDRO to divide the 401(k) account could be a winning strategy. He was relieved of the responsibility to make any payments to her and deal with tax consequences from her portion of the account. In turn, she did not have to depend on him to make quarterly payments and retained the ability to complete a tax-free rollover of an IRA or other tax-qualified plan.

17

Divorces at a Certain Age

Breaking the ties of marriage offers challenges for anyone. But for those with marriages extending 20 or 30 years, dissolving such an entrenched personal foundation can devastate. Finances and emotions interweave, a confluence powerful enough to wash away the basic understanding of day-to-day existence.

In the end, the equation is often simple: The longer the marriage, the more difficult the split. And years of married life do not guarantee a continued future together.

The percentage of divorced people older than 60 years of age across the nation has increased dramatically in recent decades, according to U.S. Census Bureau statistics. In 1970, 4.8% of men and 4.9% of women sixty or older were divorced or separated. By 2000, the percentage had more than doubled to 9.3% of older men and 10.3% of older women.

In 2000, 57,781 Georgia women over 60 years of age were divorced, compared to 36,354 men.

And in divorce, longer marriages often result in the most difficult cases. While Georgia divorce law makes no special exceptions for divorces occurring later in life, each case offers unique challenges for judges and juries responsible for crafting an equitable division.

Divorces after 30 years of marriage or between people age 60 and older are almost exclusively about the distribution of property. Few of these cases involve child support or visitation schedules because children usually are grown and have their own families.

Often women concern themselves most with staying in their home, while most men are focused on when they can expect a comfortable retirement.

"Women who put their jobs on hold many years ago in order to raise their children find it almost impossible to re-enter the workforce because they have no real marketable skills," says Karen Tsinikas, Certified Divorce Financial Analyst in Atlanta. "In this instance, an unequal settlement may be the most equitable settlement."

Any woman facing such a situation should consult with an attorney to project the cash flow available on assets, including equity on real estate holdings, her spouse's retirement funds, defined benefit plans, stock options and bonuses.

A husband may look at his life and conclude that he has provided enough for this woman over the years. He may believe those assets are his because he worked while she stayed home. Such a mindset can lead to difficult settlements.

Financial planners generally suggest having 70% to 80% of your pre-retirement income after you retire, but that varies with different income levels. Those in the lowest levels, who often live paycheck to paycheck, usually need 100% of pre-retirement income just to pay bills.

People at the top income levels often find themselves locked into the need for disposable income, unhappy unless surrounded by luxuries.

It's impossible, though, to plan for the unexpected. An illness can sap well-laid retirement plans, eating through nest eggs. With high stakes and great variability, it's vital to plan carefully and cautiously negotiate retirement benefits.

Social Security Benefits

Divorce often hits those dependent on Social Security the hardest, particularly if the couple required all of the joint benefits to survive. Separating the mutual income can leave either individual unable to cope.

An attorney may ask a financial advisor to evaluate such circumstances and determine if a couple can survive a split. A final effort at reconciliation might prove prudent, if difficult.

Your divorced spouse can get benefits on your Social Security record if the marriage lasted at least 10 years. Your divorced spouse must be 62 or older and unmarried.

The benefit level he or she obtains does not effect the amount of benefits you or your current spouse can expect. Also, if you and your ex-spouse have been divorced for at least two years and both are at least 62, he or she can get benefits even if you are not retired.

If your divorced spouse dies, you can receive benefits as a widow or widower if the marriage lasted 10 years or more. Benefits paid to a surviving divorced spouse who is 60 or older will not affect the benefit rates for other survivors receiving benefits.

Remarriage, though, can change the benefits plan. In general, you cannot receive survivors benefits if you remarry before the age of 60 unless the latter marriage ends, whether by death, divorce, or annulment. If you remarry after age 60 (50 if disabled), you can still collect benefits on your former spouse's record.

When you reach age 62 or older, you may get retirement benefits on the record of your new spouse if they are higher. Your remarriage would have no effect on the benefits being paid to your children.

If you are collecting survivors benefits, you can switch to your own retirement benefits (assuming you are eligible and your retirement rate is higher than the widow/widower's rate) as early as age 62. In many cases, you can begin receiving retirement benefits either on your own or your spouse's record at age 62, and then switch to the other benefit when you reach full retirement age, if that amount is higher.

To determine the available benefits under Social Security, contact the local Social Security Administration office and ask for a printout of benefits available in the future, either individually or through the other spouse. The Social Security Administration can also be contacted on the internet at www.ssa.gov. Appendix H at the end of this book contains an example of the Social Security Information Request Form that can be obtained from the local office.

S N A P S H O T

The Ultimate Loss of Identity

His View

She seemed perfect for him when they married in 1964: adventurous, funny, tall and beautiful. But somewhere between raising children and balancing work, whatever they felt for each other died. He worked long hours to support his new family, and she devoted herself to maintaining the home. He recalled taking her to the hospital, but after that, he just remembers looking up at the dinner table and realizing he had five children in either high school or college. He traveled often with his job selling employee benefit plans to small companies. When he was home, he just wanted to listen to his music and read a book.

Gradually, the children left home, which just seemed normal to him and her deep sadness at their absence surprised him.

She announced she wanted a divorce shortly after their 40th anniversary. He didn't know what to think. How long had she been unhappy? When did she stop loving him? He never stopped loving her. He always worked hard to provide for his family. That was what a good husband did. Now she was leaving, explaining that she needed to find herself before it was too late. He didn't know what that meant, but he had no choice other than to let her go.

Her View

She felt she spent married life just trying to make him happy, a chore since he never said he loved her or acknowledged her efforts. At first she thought it was her. Raising five children and taking care of the family home was sometimes more than she could handle. But she never counted on him for help. He was like an uninvited guest in her bed.

To mask her loneliness, she devoted herself to the well-being of her children. When they left, it moved her one step closer to being alone with him.

She filled her days caring for her grandchildren and volunteering two days a week at the church. She dreaded evenings at home because he was not interested in talking to her. After several months of volunteering in the church office, she was offered a full-time position. She accepted, feeling a sense of independence for the first time in decades.

He thought it was the passing of their 40th anniversary that made her want the divorce. He was wrong.

The trigger was her 60th birthday. She was trapped in a loveless marriage for her entire adult life. It was her turn to live. Her only hope for happiness was to leave him and start a new life.

The Result

The divorce physically separated two people who were already emotionally apart. He said people their age didn't get divorced, but she was determined. She was ready to live as a free and independent woman. But she could tell the divorce upset him greatly. She never meant to hurt him, but she had fallen out of love with him years ago.

After 40 years of marriage, they had their home, two cars, some antique furniture, two flexible premium insurance policies, two burial plots, a couple of small retirement accounts and many frequent flyer miles. This appeared to be their complete estate, until she told her attorney what he did for a living. The attorney found a treasure trove of residuals, the commissions companies pay brokers each time their customers pay their premiums for a new period. In many cases, the sale of insurance policies or benefit plans can produce residual income indefinitely. He didn't reveal these assets because he honestly believed she was not eligible to own them since he earned the commissions himself and they were in his name. But all income earned during the marriage and all property purchased with that income are marital assets, and they all go into a pot for division.

They submitted their property situation to mediation. Using this method, this late-in-life divorce was settled at a fraction of the cost of going to court. Since she didn't want the house, he kept it, along with some of the furniture, his car and his insurance policy. If she didn't want to live with him, she surely didn't want to stay with him through eternity, so she left him the burial plots. She took her car, the rest of the furniture, her insurance policy, a portion of his retirement money and most of the frequent flier miles. (Her children were now all over the country and she wanted to visit them.) She also took a stake in his residual income.

Their divorce was final before they celebrated their 41st wedding anniversary.

18

Marital Debt and the Impact of Bankruptcy

A couple earns money together. And a couple can go into debt together. A divorce settlement must recognize both instances, including specifically setting out the repayment of those debts.

Even though money is at the root of most marital strife, whenever possible you should work together to pay off major debts as part of the divorce settlement. The sale of the home, other real estate or personal items can often balance the finances. When there's too little cash available to accomplish that, though, the completed settlement agreement should specify who will pay which debt.

For each debt, the responsible person should promise to stand good for the obligation, covering any expenses incurred by the ex-spouse related to the debt. This process is called indemnifying your spouse against this debt.

Cataloging Your Debt

It practically goes without saying that in the case of debt, no one can simply disregard it. Ignorance is not a protection. Some spouses secretly create debt, which must be addressed before the divorce can be resolved. Couples who use a joint credit card, though, cannot really claim to be blameless about the debt.

A credit bureau report offers a good source of information about your debts, often resulting in a surprising number of debts listed in your name. Never sign a settlement agreement that specifies debt payments without completing an exhaustive review of your credit history.

Communication from a finance company often provides the news of a debt your ex-spouse created and you missed during the divorce.

Apportioning Debt

Whether you agree to split up the debt or the court orders it, the answers to the following questions can determine responsibility for a debt:

- Who retains any asset securing the debt after the divorce?
- What is the purpose of the debt?
- What are the financial prospects for the parties now and in the future?
- Is there any agreement between the parties concerning the debts?
- What is the overall apportionment of property?
- How long has the marriage lasted?

Provide your attorney with a list of all debts, including a breakdown of who incurred which ones. Also, provide a detailed list of purchases made on an account and the current status of those assets. Include the name and address of creditors, as well as account numbers.

WHICH DEBTS BELONG TO WHOM?

A vexing problem with division of assets or debts is ambiguity. A settlement agreement should not merely define the amount of debt, note the ones targeted for payment and generally split responsibility for the others. The agreement must specify the particular debts and their amounts, and how to dispose of them.

Consider paying off as many debts as possible. Cancel the accounts or convert them into the name of one spouse during the divorce. You can also agree to refinance debts within a certain time to remove your name from the obligation. The other spouse must, however, qualify for refinancing.

An irresponsible spouse can damage the other's credit rating during and after the divorce, something the settlement negotiations should consider. To reach a settlement, parties may agree to divide the joint debts in some manner. The attorneys should include language in the agreement that the party responsible for a debt indemnifies and holds the other party harmless for the debt.

If neither person has substantial assets, or if incomes are nearly equal, you may wind up sharing the debt load. Each person can make payments to specific creditors while trying to sell an asset such as the home and use the proceeds from that sale to reduce or pay off joint debt.

BANKRUPTCY AND ITS EFFECT ON MARITAL DEBTS

People file for bankruptcy for many reasons: illness, loss of a job, some other temporary setback, excessive use of credit cards and divorce. Often bankruptcy allows someone to avoid repayment of a portion of outstanding debt. Never a good option, bankruptcy once offered more strategic advantages than today.

New federal bankruptcy laws enacted in 2005 created a complex and fundamental change to the legal code focused on requiring more people to repay more debt. A Chapter 7 filing once wiped most debt clean, for example, but the new rules evaluate a person's ability to repay even in this form of bankruptcy. The new law provides a system of means testing to determine how much a person can repay and sets a higher standard for qualifying for Chapter 7.

For many couples, bankruptcy once often came with divorce, either because of a lack of money to pay off debts or when one spouse decided to use it as a weapon, declaring bankruptcy rather than relinquishing an asset.

A bankruptcy filing might have eliminated or reduced some debts, leaving more money for the payment of ongoing expenses and often simplifying the divorce.

Under the new rules, bankruptcy only rarely provides a clearly beneficial option, says Shayna Steinfeld, an Atlanta attorney certified in bankruptcy. "It pretty much says bankruptcy can no longer be a tool in a divorce case," she says.

Individual exceptions may exist, so consult carefully with your attorney. Make sure bankruptcy is your only option, and don't expect to simply make your debts disappear by filing.

It's a lesson people are still learning. "I still get calls from people thinking they can get out of a property settlement by filing Chapter 7, so the word is not out there yet," Steinfeld says.

In some cases, you may file under Chapter 13, which requires repayment of debt over three to five years, to wrangle over property and delay or avoid a property division. After reviewing the details, few people have historically found this to be a compelling option, Steinfeld says. "In most divorces, bankruptcy is simply no longer a realistic tool. You can still consider it, but it's not the cure-all it used to be."

If one person chooses to file for bankruptcy alone, however, family law and bankruptcy law can become entangled. Fortunately, the bankruptcy code attempts to protect the rights of children and former spouses by considering support — whether child support or alimony — as priority claims that must be paid and may not be discharged under any bankruptcy chapter. This makes it much harder for the spouse who filed bankruptcy to avoid contempt actions for on-going support payments. Also, bankruptcy may make it possible for the person owed alimony or child support to recover past-due support by liquidating property otherwise exempt from division.

ALTERNATIVES TO BANKRUPTCY

Ideally, everyone has the resources to pay all the bills each month. But the world is not perfect or people would not divorce. Dividing a financially stable household into two single-income households with comparable expenses can lead to the realization that, despite all best efforts, the means do not meet the ends.

While calls from creditors or collection agents cause people to consider bankruptcy, other options offer answers, and maybe even a way to save a person's credit rating.

Establish a home equity line of credit — Real property tends to appreciate in value. A common source of money to pay off debts is a home equity line of credit. Most are available for up to 80% of a home's value, and in some cases the interest is tax deductible.

Renegotiate secured loans — Loans secured by homes and automobiles are often the largest debts. Consider negotiating a lower interest rate on a home loan and refinancing to save several hundred dollars monthly. Extending the loan over a longer period can reduce monthly payments, although you often pay substantially more in interest over the life of the loan.

Renegotiate unsecured loans — Lenders realize bankruptcy can severely affect unsecured loans. Often, they eagerly compromise. Some merchants will reduce or eliminate interest or carrying charges to recover the principal.

Defer the debt — With unsecured loans, such as revolving charge accounts, the creditor may allow a grace period in order to keep a good customer and recover the money.

Ask for reduced interest — Creditors may not reduce the principal, but many will reduce the interest on a loan.

Consolidate your debts — Some traditional lenders offer loans to consolidate debts into one manageable payment at a reasonable interest rate. Talk with a personal banker for additional information. Avoid transferring balances between credit cards. While many cards offer teaser rates to induce such transfers, consumers often get caught rolling the debt between cards, incurring unnecessary finance and interest charges and managing an ever-increasing debt load.

Seek credit counseling — These agencies provide an additional alternative in the absence of traditional lending options, although you should be wary of for-profit companies that sometimes take your money and fail to apply it to your debts.

The Consumer Credit Counseling Service (CCCS), with offices throughout Greater Atlanta, is a non-profit organization that sponsors a debt management program to repay debts by restructuring a budget and negotiating with creditors.

Creditors often reduce interest and finance charges for CCCS program participants. The one monthly payment is typically less than payments to individual creditors. Plans can pay off obligations in as little as three years, a substantially shorter time than making the minimum monthly payment on the same obligations.

Part Three

Look to the Future

S N A P S H O T

NO CLEAR LINK BETWEEN CHILD SUPPORT AND VISITATION

His View

He knew he wasn't the best husband. As a father, though, he didn't deserve punishment. She should have expected tough times when she took their kids and left him. Working as a finish carpenter, how could he pay child support and have anything left to live on?

From day one of the marriage, they fought. Being broke all the time annoyed her. He liked to have a few drinks and kept late nights. She and the kids seemed okay.

After four years of misery, she moved out, which was fine with him. He could see his kids when he wanted and didn't have to worry about the day-to-day hassles.

In the divorce settlement, they agreed to joint custody. Still, the kids lived with her most of the time. He paid child support and had visitation rights. They agreed to equally split certain expenses for the children. She sent him a monthly itemized list outlining the child support obligations. She paid these expenses and he reimbursed her for his part.

At first, he sent the money every month, though he had other priorities. And since she was already paying for everything, he figured she could cover the basics even if he didn't contribute.

He tried to keep the schedule but an accident on the job left him unable to pay child support for a couple of months. Afterward, she refused to give him time with the kids. That's when he realized their importance to him.

While he didn't want to take her to court, it was worth it if he could see his children more. After his first meeting with his attorney, he knew his only hope was to take his ex-wife to court.

180

Her View

Giving birth to a son changed her life forever, ending the chase with her husband for the good times. They needed to get serious and after the birth of their daughter she realized his wild ways and lack of ambition wouldn't go away.

She tried to make it work but finally gave up and moved into an apartment barely big enough for her and the kids. Initially, she thought her job was enough but she didn't realize two children could cost so much. Each month, she worried herself sick and waited until she was desperate before calling him. She hated having to do it. He was always eager to see the kids, but he seemed to give more excuses than child support.

How could he not provide for the children he claimed to love? She finally told him he couldn't see the kids unless he helped provide.

The Result

They launched a battle over child support and visitation. The judge slammed him for spending too much of his money on good times and too little on his children. The judge held him in contempt of court for failing to pay child support in a timely fashion. His ex-wife felt pretty good hearing all of this, until the judge held her in contempt for denying him visitation. While both child support and visitation are vital matters, they are independent of each other, the judge said.

The judge ordered him to pay a specific amount of child support each month and warned her against restricting his access to the children.

19

Support Your Children

Divorce never ends your responsibility to a child, particularly at a time when a child's emotions are often the most raw, and his or her needs most critical. While no one should shirk the financial responsibilities, child support is unfortunately the debt often left unpaid.

In Georgia alone, 346,008 child support cases showed payments in arrears in 2006, according to one federal report. And the federal government estimates that payment of all child support nationwide could lift almost all children out of poverty in this country.

Some child support, however, goes unpaid for legitimate reasons when those obligated to pay lose jobs or suffer from physical or mental problems that limit their capacity to earn.

But the vast majority of what we call deadbeat parents simply refuse to pay their obligations, choosing to remain purposely underemployed, spending money on themselves or supporting only their new families.

"Too many parents involve their children in the support debate, and that's always destructive," says Atlanta counselor Lawrence C. Adams. "A parent may put a child in the position of message bearer, often saying that the mother doesn't have enough money or asking why they have to suffer. Those messages are almost always initiated by a spouse who feels the settlement is unfair."

A failure to pay child support can create financial insecurity in both the recipient spouse and the children as well as an impending sense that the payor spouse is disengaging from the kids.

CHILD SUPPORT COLLECTION

Powerful forces work against deadbeat parents. The federal government created the Parent Locator Service to harness the resources of the Social Security Administration and the Internal Revenue Service to locate a non-paying parent or his or her employer. Once the parent is found, the custodial parent can enforce a child support order signed by the judge and collect unpaid support.

In Georgia, the Department of Human Resources' Office of Child Support Services bears responsibility for collections on a state level. The agency can assist with locating noncustodial parents, confirming paternity, establishing and enforcing child support and medical support orders, and collecting and distributing payments.

CALCULATING CHILD SUPPORT

In 2006, Georgia lawmakers updated state laws governing child support. The sweeping changes touched nearly every aspect of the issue, particularly the calculation of support. The old law primarily looked at the income of the parent obligated to pay.

The new law considers the income of both parents, a reflection of the growing number of two-income families and of joint custody arrangements.

Arguing in support of the changes, some people contend it is unfair to only consider the income of one parent. Evaluating the income of both parents responsible for the child, they believe, creates a more balanced and fair support decision. Others, though, question if the new law will dramatically reduce the amount of support payments and put more stress on the parent tending to the child. The new law went into effect in January 2007, and time will be needed to weigh the law's practical application.

As with many aspects of a Georgia divorce, the state provided only broad guidelines. Judges and juries retain discretion based on evidence presented during the divorce to adjust child support awards. The duration of child support continues until a minor child reaches the age of majority, which is 18 in Georgia. Exceptions generally include the child's death, marriage or emancipation. The court may, at its discretion, order support to continue for a child who has not completed secondary education by age 18, but that support ends at age 20.

Calculating support begins with identifying the gross income of each parent, including salaries, commissions, bonuses and capital gains. It's a complex equation illustrated by how the law handles issues such as self-employment income or fringe benefits.

For the self-employed, the calculation must consider income against reasonable expenses of self-employment or business operations needed to produce income. Excessive promotional costs, travel, vehicle or personal living expenses are not considered reasonable and could count as income.

Similarly, employment fringe benefits considered to significantly reduce personal living expenses count as income. So, a court could consider a company car, housing or room and board as part of an individual's income, weighing it as a factor in child support.

While the calculation includes many forms of income, other money remains exempt. Child support payments received for the benefit of a child of another relationship do not count as income. Also, assistance programs such as food stamps or state aid programs don't figure into the calculation.

Once a court weighs all of the variables, the result is an adjusted gross income calculation. The judge or jury must make certain adjustments to the parent's gross income based on pre-existing child support orders, self employment and Medicare taxes as well as the other children living in a parent's household to whom the parent owes a duty of support.

Also, anyone who hopes to avoid payment by taking a lower-paying job faces a risk. The court, under a similarly comprehensive evaluation, can determine if a parent is voluntarily unemployed or underemployed and factor that into an award.

After calculation of the adjusted gross income, child support is based on the combined adjusted monthly income of the two parents. Georgia law provides detailed examples for a range of income extending from $800 monthly to $30,000 monthly. Here is a sampling of guidelines for the base-line child support:

Monthly Income	Payment: One Child	Payment: Two Children
$4,000	$779	$1,104
$8,000	$1,125	$1,567
$12,500	$1,466	$2,035

After determining each parent's child support obligation under the table, the judge or jury is required to consider additional expenses for work-related child care costs and insurance premiums in its calculations to determine actual child support obligations. Moreover, the amount of child support owed may be deviated upwards or downwards by the judge or jury based on certain factors including but not limited to high or low income, travel, mortgage expense, extraordinary medical and educational expenses as well as extended parenting time with the noncustodial parent or when the child resides with both parents equally.

Failing to pay child support can cause financial damage. In Georgia, the amount of a missed payment begins to accrue 7% per annum interest 30 days after the payment's due date. Obviously, the cost of missing a payment can rise quickly.

Also, the person owed the payment faces no obligation to accept less money than the original payment plus the penalties. An ex who owes cannot simply entice a former spouse to accept a guaranteed payment of the original amount in return for forgetting about the penalty. In instances of hardship, some flexibility is built into the system. The court can reduce or waive the penalty based on an evaluation of considerations such as substantial hardship and the parent's past reliability for payment. The court, though, can also weigh a reduction against any possible harm to the parent owed the money.

Georgia makes the bottom line very clear. A parent must support his or her children, regardless of the divorce.

20

Insuring Your Health and Life

In Georgia, about 13% of the population, or one million people, under the age of 64 are uninsured, according to the
Georgia Healthcare Coverage Project. Of the entire population
of 8.5 million people, 18% were uninsured for at least one month
during the year evaluated.

The healthcare project, created as a non-partisan forum to
build consensus on healthcare issues, found that participation in
health coverage plans varies by region, with rural areas lagging
the state's metropolitan areas.

If both parties in a Georgia divorce work and their employers
offer health coverage, they may escape becoming among the uninsured. If one person does not have a job, works for an employer
who offers no coverage or is covered by the spouse's insurance
during the marriage, this issue needs close consideration in the
settlement agreement.

HEALTH INSURANCE FOR THE CHILDREN

Georgia courts wish to protect the health of children whose parents divorce. As with child support, the state's lawmakers recommend guidelines for the state's courts, and the state offers an additional safety net for children.

The PeachCare for Kids program provides comprehensive health care for uninsured children. Benefits include primary, preventive, specialist, dental care and vision care. The program also includes hospitalization, emergency room services, prescription medications and mental health care.

Uninsured children younger than 19 qualify for the program if their families earn less than or equal to 235% of the federal poverty limit, or about $47,000 for a family of four. About 247,000 children were enrolled in the program as of March 2006. The state program, though, does not absolve a parent from responsibility. Far from it.

The parent obligated to pay child support is generally required to provide major medical insurance for a minor child. In most cases, health insurance is available through the obligated spouse's employment.

The court, though, retains flexibility, and the goal is to provide the greatest amount of coverage for children of divorce. For example, the court must decide if accident and sickness coverage is available to the obligated spouse at reasonable cost. However, the court may weigh if the spouse receiving child support can retain health coverage through employment or other group plans at a reasonable price. The court may order coverage under that parent's plan, with the obligated parent contributing to the cost at a certain level.

As anyone familiar with health insurance knows, some expenses are not always covered. Both parents generally bear responsibility for uninsured health care expenses, which are paid based on a proportion determined by the court.

Each parent must pay in a timely manner or risk exposure to additional legal action by the other spouse.

While the goal is simple—protecting the children—the specifics are complicated. Spend time with your attorney to make sure you understand all of the ramifications and obligations for keeping your children healthy.

HEALTH INSURANCE FOR YOUR SPOUSE

Most health insurance plans will not allow one spouse to retain coverage for the other after the divorce. A spouse needing coverage can look to the following options:

Coverage through an employer — The spouse may not have selected this coverage before the divorce because it may not be the best coverage or come at a high price. Obtaining coverage through an employer, though, is usually more affordable than other options.

COBRA (Consolidated Omnibus Budget Reconciliation Act) — If an employer plan discontinues coverage, this federal program provides coverage for a limited time. Administered through the employer, COBRA should offer the same benefits as the employer plan at a slightly higher premium. Each spouse should check with the employer to confirm availability of this coverage before final resolution of the case.

Individual plan — A spouse who is relatively young and in good physical condition may qualify for an individual policy sold by a company representative or insurance broker. Expect these policies to cost more and offer less coverage than group plans.

Take special care if one spouse has a major pre-existing condition such as cancer or heart disease, which a new, post-divorce insurance policy might not cover. Examine this possibility and assess the costs associated with medical care.

The expense associated with cancer or other major illnesses can play a large role in a person's financial needs, and place limits on the ability to earn a living. As a result, some people may dispute the severity of health conditions due to the potential implications.

These may be good-faith claims that could seem completely reasonable and be accepted by the other spouse under different circumstances. But people naturally become suspicious of the other side during a divorce, and they may feel they cannot properly evaluate the burdens they are undertaking. For instance, the spouse obligated to pay child support may claim an on-the-job back injury, restricting work and the payment of child support. The other spouse may deny the injury, claiming an attempt to escape responsibility.

The obligated spouse's attorney can hire a physician to assess the situation, and expert medical witnesses are expensive. Don't consider such an investment unless a large amount of money is at stake. The spouse could significantly reduce the cost of such a move by gathering all medical records related to the condition for the lawyer to review. Otherwise, the lawyer may have to subpoena the medical records at considerable expense.

Life Insurance Protects Future Payments

No one can ignore the inevitable. Planning for the death of a parent or spouse makes wise financial sense. For example, what happens if the parent paying significant child support dies? Life insurance should cover the ongoing obligations to the children.

That's only one example, though. Parents should consider a range of scenarios, says Kirk Wimberly, a life insurance professional with the Northwestern Mutual Financial Network, Estate Strategies Group, in Atlanta.

What if one parent is a ne'er-do-well with no resources and the responsible parent dies. The responsible parent's life insurance had better be sufficient to care for the children, who may have no other resources, Wimberly says.

Careful planning is as critical on the opposite end of the economic spectrum. "We often sit down with someone and say, 'Just what would you want to be accomplished after you died?' They would like to pay off the mortgage on their home in Sandy Springs; they'd like to be sure that each of their children has the opportunity to go to Emory; they'd like to have some money in the bank for emergencies; a sister and brother-in-law would probably raise the children, but they'd certainly need the wherewithal to do that," Wimberly says.

In such a case, a careful analysis of the individual's finances would determine if he or she might need to purchase additional life insurance.

Also, insurance is relatively inexpensive, although age matters. "If we are talking about an older parent in their 50s, then it's a different price than a parent in their late 20s. But still, it's amazingly inexpensive to get a half-million dollars of capital, or a more common amount in today's world would be a million to $3 million. For $100 a month, you can probably generate an amazing amount of capital, and then consequently, a significant income to children if something happened to you," Wimberly says.

In instances of divorce, when the welfare of a child may hinge on a parent's financial foundation, making good decisions regarding insurance is critical.

Helping Her Regain Her Balance

<u>Her View</u>

She never intended to stay home after the birth of their first child. He pushed it. She weighed so many reasons for her to continue working against the one reason to stay home. She agonized over the decision for months. But in the end, she decided to leave her job.

Staying home presented a difficult transition. She filled her days with household chores, chasing after her son and making sure dinner was ready. She was lonely. She clung to her husband as her only portal to the outside world. He seemed so unsympathetic to her needs and her growing depression.

On several occasions, she approached him about returning to work. He would not consider the idea. Her place was at home.

They began to argue, mostly about money. She never saw the family checkbook. He only told her whether or not she exceeded her weekly budget.

It was his need to control her. They never talked, never spent time together as a couple and she felt her marriage slipping away. She quietly began to collect financial information and contacted an attorney. She wanted out.

She knew years of staying home diminished her earning capacity. She told her attorney that alimony was not a mere option; it was a priority. She couldn't get back on her feet without it.

His View

He was excited when the baby came, and he always wanted a son. But he was adamant that a stranger would not raise his child. She would have to stay home. Carrying the weight of the family was stressful, and she didn't help the situation. She complained constantly about loneliness and her whining frustrated him. She didn't realize what a privilege it was for her to stay home while other women balanced so much in their lives. All she had to do was take care of one child and keep the house clean.

He gave her a generous weekly allowance, but somehow each week she spent more. Life is filled with trade-offs, and she couldn't spend money like she did when she had a job. Her answer to the problem was to return to work.

But she refused to see his point of view, and he could not understand why it was so difficult for her. Her depression affected every facet of their marriage. He was seriously thinking about separating to see if she would come to her senses.

When he suggested the idea, she agreed and told him she had already spoken to an attorney about a divorce. He felt betrayed.

The Result

Their separation and divorce was marred by accusations. She called him controlling for keeping her at home. He said she was unappreciative of the freedom he allowed her. They agreed on joint legal custody of their son. They split their personal property easily enough, but the division of other assets, mostly their home and his retirement account, was more difficult. It shouldn't have been, since their needs and wants worked hand in hand. She was concerned about her future. Over the time she spent at home, her job skills eroded and technology passed her by. To earn enough money, she needed additional training at a vocational school or local college.

He decided one of them needed to stay in their home, for their son. He was the one who could afford it, but he couldn't stay there and give her half the home equity and half of his retirement account.

So they worked out a plan that included rehabilitative alimony of $2,500 a month for three years in addition to child support. She used the money to move into an apartment and go to school.

21

Alimony

Yes, alimony is awarded in Georgia. The courts take alimony very seriously, although Georgia is trending more toward the national model that places a greater emphasis on the use of property division to take the place of such payments. The shift acknowledges the ability of both spouses to earn future income. The courts now tend to favor a clear division of assets and diminished ongoing payments. Of course, the parties can agree to alimony as part of a comprehensive property settlement.

Short of agreement, though, nothing is guaranteed. In all cases, the court may consider alimony but a judge or jury faces no requirement to grant support. Again, a judge or jury has great discretion, with one important exception.

If the court determines the cause of the separation falls to adultery or desertion, the offending spouse cannot receive alimony.

This holds even if a judge or jury bases approval of a divorce on other factors, requiring the court to evaluate desertion or adultery separately when considering alimony. Each spouse may present evidence as the court weighs this critical issue.

Temporary Alimony

You don't have to wait until your divorce concludes to receive alimony, and if you are the obligor parent you're not likely to avoid paying while the divorce is ongoing. While waiting for a court date or during mediation, either party may ask the presiding judge to issue temporary alimony. The court can grant alimony and include expenses connected to the litigation. In such a case, the judge should consider the necessities of each person and any evidence of a separate estate owned by either spouse.

When considering a petition for temporary alimony, the judge does not necessarily weigh the merits of the overall case. Instead, the judge may inquire into the need for temporary alimony. The judge also has the discretion to completely refuse temporary alimony.

Permanent Alimony

Similarly, the court may grant permanent alimony, ongoing payments from one spouse to the other. While labeled permanent, this form of payment usually ends at some point. All obligations to pay alimony generally stop with the remarriage of the person owed the alimony.

Permanent alimony is possible in instances of divorce, voluntary separation, and abandonment. And failing to pay can result in a contempt of court violation.

The judge or jury can consider several factors when weighing the appropriateness and amount of alimony, including the following:

- The standard of living established during the marriage
- Duration of the marriage
- The age and the physical and emotional condition of both parties
- The financial resources of each party
- Where applicable, the time necessary for either party to acquire sufficient education or training to enable that party to find appropriate employment
- The contribution of each party to the marriage, including, but not limited to, services rendered in homemaking childcare, education, and career building of the other party.
- Condition of the parties, including the separate estate, earning capacity, and fixed liabilities of the parties
- Any other factors the court deems equitable and proper

Tax Implications

Under the Internal Revenue Code, alimony or spousal maintenance payments may be a deduction for the spouse paying alimony and income to the spouse receiving the money. To qualify for alimony tax treatment, alimony or separate maintenance payments must meet all of the following requirements:

- You and your spouse or former spouse do not file a joint return.
- You pay in cash, including checks or money orders.
- The divorce or separation instrument does not say that the payment is not alimony.
- If legally separated under a decree of divorce or separate maintenance, you and your former spouse are not members of the same household when you make the payment.
- You have no liability to make any payment (in cash or property) after the death of your spouse or former spouse.
- Your payment is not treated as child support.

If you receive alimony, you must report the full amount as income on tax Form 1040. Also, child support is never deductible. If your divorce decree or settlement calls for alimony and child support, and you pay less than the total required, the IRS considers the payments first to apply as non-deductible child support. Any remaining amount is then considered alimony. Property settlements, even if required by the divorce decree, do not meet the IRS definition of alimony.

IMPACT OF BANKRUPTCY

Once again, alimony and child support cannot be discharged in bankruptcy. These are two of only a handful of debt types that must be paid regardless of whether or not a person declares bankruptcy.

Absurd Statements
Your Divorce
Lawyer Should Correct

Here's a collection of show stoppers and deal break-
ers that can put a divorce off track. Several of these
comments, of course, deal with the financial aspects of
divorce. The following is a selection of the comments
and the rationales behind them:

....

*"I'll give her $100,000 when the divorce is final, but make it
alimony so I can deduct it."*

The Internal Revenue Code prohibits disguising a
property settlement as contractual alimony. Under IRS
rules, such alimony cannot be front-loaded, but must be
paid out in at least three calendar years.

....

*"I really don't want to spend the money to conduct discovery. I
have a pretty good idea that his inventory looks about right."*

You may assume that you have accurate information
about asset values and liabilities. If you fail to use the

most often utilized means of discovery—interrogatories, requests for admission, depositions—you may be left to interpret values. This is especially true with the holdings in a pension plan. You might have seen the tax value and believe you know values, but present-day values may be quite different.

....

"Get this divorce over now. I just put a contract on a new house."

Here is where the attorney should tell you to slow down. Too often, divorcing people get in a hurry and mistakenly create marital property when that's not what they intended.

....

"My fiancé knows what I own, there really isn't any need for me to have to attach a financial statement to the prenuptial agreement" or *"My fiancé knows that I don't make much or really own anything of value, there's no reason for me to make any statements in the prenuptial agreement about those things."*

Under Georgia law, the single most important consideration for enforcement of a prenuptial agreement is whether there has been full financial disclosure. This includes income, assets and liabilities.

22

Common Tax Issues

By now you realize there are many factors critical to creating a financially secure and prudent divorce settlement, as well as the need to understand every detail of a court-ordered decree. Few items are more important than taxes. And no matter who handled tax duties during the marriage, both spouses carry the responsibility for filing accurate returns.

Similarly, the specifics of a divorce, even the date to conclude a divorce, can create pronounced tax ripples. In fact, failing to consider those specifics during the division of property can create significant long-term imbalances. Also, remember Georgia has a 6% state income tax, whose guidelines generally follow those of the federal income tax code.

Atlanta CPA Lyn Reagan often tells clients, "In a divorce, we have to take a certain amount of money and fill three buckets: that of the moneyed spouse, one for the non-moneyed spouse (or maybe they're both making money), and that money bucket for the kids. To me those are three separate buckets. And when you go from one household to two households ... you can't run two households for the same amount as you run one; it just doesn't work."

Keeping all of the buckets balanced can include the use of several tax strategies, and most people can benefit greatly from professional advice.

"Even though assets pass from one spouse to the other without tax consequences in a divorce, there can be tremendous tax consequences later on," Reagan says. "Not the day of the transfer, because the government allows you not to have to pay ... if the husband gives the wife the house, there are no taxes to pay. But down the road, there are significant tax consequences. It takes somebody to look at that to make sure that the recipient is getting his or her fair share."

Even before developing a tax strategy, it's critical to understand the associated responsibility. No spouse should ever jeopardize his or her tax situation through ignorance.

With e-filing of income tax returns, one person can file without ever getting the signature of the other spouse. Instead, couples should discuss their return with a CPA, a good idea even for a happy couple who is not contemplating divorce. What, for example, if your spouse dies? You should understand the economics of the family's taxes.

Before the late 1990s, a spouse who blindly signed the tax return was equally responsible for errors or outright fraud. The IRS now allows someone to request innocent spouse relief. If approved, you might avoid penalties if your spouse improperly reported items or omitted items on your tax return.

"It's very difficult to get innocent spouse relief," Reagan says. "It's very important for the innocent spouse to realize that if the husband, for example, doesn't have money to pay the taxes, the IRS will come after her. Even if they're divorced."

Again, the rules are complicated. Consider this example from the IRS.

> *At the time you signed your joint return, you knew that your spouse did not report $5,000 of gambling winnings. The IRS examined your tax return several months after you filed it and determined that your spouse's unreported gambling winnings were actually $25,000. You established that you had no reason to know about the additional $20,000 because of the way your spouse handled gambling winnings. The understatement of tax due to the $20,000 will qualify for innocent spouse relief if you meet the other requirements. The understatement of tax due to the $5,000 of gambling winnings does not qualify for relief.*

Deciding exactly who is liable when a tax return goes astray demands an expert touch. Consider consulting with a professional tax advisor if there are questions. And remember, take responsibility to learn as much as possible about the household finances to avoid unwelcome IRS surprises.

PRIOR YEAR LIABILITIES OR REFUND

The settlement agreement should specify which party is responsible for prior year tax liabilities, in the event of a deficiency, or who receives a refund, in the case of an overpayment. Such a provision can protect you even if the error is not discovered until after the divorce. This is especially important when only one spouse operates a business and the other spouse has no idea about the legitimacy of deductions that spouse takes. Taxpayers filing jointly are each liable for any tax, interest or penalties associated with that return. The agreement should indemnify the spouse who is not responsible, although the IRS will attempt to collect from either party.

Such tax issues are overlooked by a vast majority of divorcing people. The spouse who has the return prepared has a great deal of control over possible refunds. Overpayment of taxes by someone preparing the return is also a popular way to hide money in a divorce.

"It happens all the time," Reagan says. Consider a husband who manages the bills. He may choose to write a $25,000 check to the IRS from a joint $100,000 savings account, hoping a cursory analysis of the savings account will show a lesser value of $75,000 in the account. When he files taxes after the divorce, the IRS will return the overpayment of $25,000 and he may avoid having that money included in the division of assets.

A careful analysis of the accounts, though, should identify such actions, and no one should ignore this in-depth review. A final hedge against such a maneuver is a requirement in a settlement agreement that any refund be split between the parties and not credited to just one spouse.

WHO FILES CURRENT YEAR TAX RETURN?

While married couples living together typically file joint returns, divorced spouses must file separately, often leading to higher tax brackets and larger tax burdens. The tax status of a taxpayer is determined as of the end of the tax year. If a couple divorces on December 31, they cannot file a joint return for that year. If tax savings are significant, consider entering into a settlement agreement before the end of the year with the divorce decree finalized after New Year's Day.

One or both spouses may have lower income tax costs from filing as married rather than single. If the divorce is amicable enough to make a delay possible, the spouse with the higher income may consider accelerating income into the current tax year and delaying deductions until the following year. Such a move could lower your overall taxes.

PAYMENTS AND TRANSFERS

Property transfers from one spouse to another in connection with a divorce are nontaxable events. Neither party realizes a gain or loss for income tax purposes with the transfer of property as part of the allocation of assets in their divorce. But there may be future tax consequences from the division of assets. For example, say a couple divorces with only two assets: 500 shares of stock with a current market value of $50,000 and a $50,000 certificate of deposit. Since the CD is a form of cash, its tax basis is always equal to the stated value of the CD because the tax basis of cash is simply the amount of cash.

The tax basis of the stock, on the other hand, may be different from its current value. If the stock appreciates substantially, its tax basis may be much less than its current market value. In our example, if you purchased the stock four months before the divorce for $20,000, you have a potential gain of $30,000 now that it is worth $50,000.

In this example, the person receiving the CD would realize $50,000 from the divorce allocation, but the other spouse would ultimately realize something less than $50,000 when the stock is sold and taxes paid.

When each person is in a different marginal tax bracket, you might consider transferring marital property with a larger built-in gain to the spouse in the lower tax bracket. You could transfer marital property with little or no gain, or that may have actually declined in value, to the spouse in the higher tax bracket.

Let's say a divorcing couple divided much of their property, leaving a lake house and some stocks. The market value of the stock is approximately the same as the equity in the house. Giving one person the stock and the other the house may seem equal, except that the two assets could have widely differing tax bases. Since the husband is retired and in a much lower marginal tax bracket than the wife, who is still working, it might be equitable for the husband to receive the asset with the greater potential tax gain. Property arrangements are so complex and subject to so many variables that you need to check them out with a tax expert.

WHO CAN TAKE ADVANTAGE OF DEPENDENCY EXEMPTIONS?

Many people will enjoy a greater tax benefit by filing as head of household rather than someone filing singly or even as married and filing separately. To receive this status, you must only prove you provide a home for a child for more than six months of the year, Reagan says. Also, you do not have to claim the child as a dependent to file as head of household.

"It's a more favorable tax bracket, so you pay less taxes," she says. This often proves beneficial in custody arrangements involving two children who live an equal amount of time in each parent's home. Both parents, claiming one child as a six-month resident, could claim head of household status.

The trial court has no authority to award the federal tax dependency exemption to a noncustodial parent. The dependency exemption is dictated by the Internal Revenue Code, which grants the exemption to the parent having custody of the child for the greater portion of the year, unless the parties agree otherwise.

If the parents agree to equal periods of possession, the decree should specify that one of the spouses file IRS Form 8332 to let the government know who will claim the kids. If there is more than one child, the parents may agree to divide the dependency exemptions. If there is only one child, the parents may alternate the claim.

When negotiating tax exemptions, make sure you don't waste them. That is possible if they go to a parent with too little or too much income. You must have income from which to deduct the amount of the exemption. Without income, there is no deduction.

Similarly, you can waste the child exemption on the rich. For people who make over a certain threshold, which changes each year, personal exemptions begin to phase out and are completely without benefit at a certain amount.

The benefit does not end when a child goes to college, since a parent must maintain a residence for the child's return. Consult with your tax advisor to understand the specifics of this often beneficial strategy.

RETIREMENT PLAN ISSUES

As detailed earlier, you can divide a retirement plan as part of the settlement and avoid tax consequences by entering a Qualified Domestic Relations Order (QDRO). A QDRO basically divides one plan into two, leaving a portion in the name of the original owner and transferring the remaining portion into an IRA in the name of the other spouse.

Most employers will immediately distribute the non-employee spouse's portion of a defined contribution plan (e.g., a 401(k) or savings plan) to that spouse. The non-employee spouse may choose to either roll this distribution over into an IRA account or take possession of the assets.

If the non-employee spouse takes possession of the assets, income taxes apply but not tax penalties. A distribution from the account at divorce is one of the few instances where retirement assets can be prematurely distributed from a qualified plan without having to pay the penalty.

If the original owner withdraws money from the plan during the divorce or just before the separation, the settlement agreement should specify that this person is responsible for tax consequences associated with the withdrawal. If the parties agree to file a joint tax return as part of the divorce settlement, address the responsibility for income taxes associated with that withdrawal. Transfer of an individual retirement account (IRA) or individual retirement annuity during the divorce is not a taxable transfer. A QDRO is not necessary to divide or transfer interest in an IRA.

Overpayment of Taxes

A clever way to hide assets is pre-payment of taxes. For example, a divorcing couple might be owed a large income tax refund and one spouse might apply it to the next year's tax liability with the intention of applying it only to his or her taxes. Make certain your spouse does not use this method to significantly alter his or her income tax withholding.

Account statements for payments made in the current or prior tax years can be obtained easily from your local IRS office if the payments are made in the names of both spouses. If payments are made separately, your spouse must sign an IRS form authorizing you to have this information.

The other spouse might also prepay property taxes on a home and then negotiate for possession of that home.

Taxing Closely Held Businesses

Be sure to address the tax liabilities associated with a business and the sources of income a party may receive from a closely held business. The IRS may allow a business to take deductions that are appropriate for tax purposes. But the divorce court may consider these deductions as income to a particular spouse for purposes of calculating child support or valuing the company. They include retirement plan contributions, company cars, insurance benefits, travel benefits, travel reimbursements and personal expenditures made by the company on behalf of you or your spouse. Consult with an accountant and other necessary professionals on the various problems associated with a closely held business. Since the IRS may request an audit, make certain your agreement includes the necessary protective language.

23

Your Relationship With the Court System

Even though most divorce cases settle, one feature inherent in Georgia law makes going to court potentially difficult: any Georgian can request a jury to hear a divorce case.

THE FAMILY COURT SETUP IN GEORGIA

Divorces in Georgia are typically heard in the superior court of the couple's residence county. The only court designated specifically for family law is a pilot program in Fulton County. Other counties are free to set their own rules, with some assigning a junior or senior judge to hear cases or rotating the responsibility among judges. While Georgia does have broad laws establishing the court system, each county court may develop many of its own practices and policies. As a result, the experience of going through a divorce often varies from county to county.

Your First Court Setting

No matter where your divorce is filed, eventually it goes on the court's trial calendar if you are unable to reach agreement through mediation or some other method. The first court setting, though, often considers preliminary matters such as temporary support or who lives where during the case. This hearing usually takes place within four to six weeks of filing for divorce.

The case then goes onto the court docket. A case is often re-set more than once before actually reaching trial. Continuances, the postponement of a trial, occur for a variety of reasons: the parties may not be ready to try the case, the attorneys or their clients may have conflicting schedules or the court may have a full docket. Your case may also receive a continuance if the judge is already in trial on another case, has an immediate issue to address or an older case to hear.

Consider if one spouse must sell assets or transfer them to the other spouse to finalize the divorce. The spouse who will have to pay may want the case continued for as long as possible. In some cases, the receiving spouse then becomes anxious to settle—even to the point of accepting an inadequate offer—because the other side successfully delays the trial and keeps the assets in limbo. A spouse may also want to slow the divorce if the other spouse will receive significant compensation in the near future, such as a bonus or the proceeds from a sale. Factor in the expenses associated with delay to see if settling immediately outweighs the advantages of a greater settlement later.

Though settlement happens in the vast majority of cases, some divorce cases simply must be adjudicated in court, particularly those involving a matter of principle or a broad disagreement involving intense animosity. There are a lot of games played by divorcing couples over the threat of court. When one spouse believes the other lacks the intestinal fortitude to risk the courtroom, that spouse will often finagle his or her way into a protracted series of delays. Show your spouse you will stand up for yourself before, during and after the divorce and, in the long run, you will simplify your life. If you will not be bullied, the bully loses his or her power.

APPEARING IN COURT

On the morning you are scheduled in court, take the experience seriously. Dress with a respect for the system. Men should wear a suit or sport coat with slacks, a white or pastel shirt and a tie. A nice dress or suit is appropriate for a woman. If you're not sure about your wardrobe choices, consult your attorney. Image is important when speaking to a judge or jury. In a marital dispute involving finances, your credibility is on the line from the start. Your appearance should communicate that you are worthy of a successful outcome.

Remember to set a place to meet your attorney at the courthouse. Judges are assigned their own courtrooms and the most likely place to meet is in a nearby hallway. To reach many courtrooms, you must pass through a metal detector. Do not carry anything possibly considered a weapon or that might set off the alarm, including mace canisters, heavy key chains or a letter opener.

When you appear in court, always act in a mature and professional manner. Emotion-fueled threats, even violence, have marred family court actions in this state over the years. Judges who see this type of behavior clamp down with a zero tolerance policy and can snatch one of the parties from the courtroom into a holding cell or under supervision.

Always approach your day in court with a calm, cool exterior, even if a swarm of butterflies turn flips in your stomach. Many cases settle because one party appears so confident in court that he or she scares the other side. As in most things in life, the individual who keeps the emotions in check often wins.

Courtroom Cast of Characters

The state organizes superior courts into 10 judicial districts made up of judicial circuits. Each county has its own superior court, but the judge may serve more than one county.

Here are the titles and functions of the people you will encounter in the courtroom:

Superior court judge — In Georgia, superior court judges are elected and serve four-year terms in non-partisan, circuit-wide races. Qualifications to serve as a superior court judge include seven years as a practicing attorney. The judge may act as the fact finder in a case or help a jury reach a decision.

Bailiff — This is a uniformed officer of the court who keeps order and enforces the wishes of the judge. If one party gets belligerent and the judge holds him or her in contempt, the bailiff takes that person to jail. In jury trials, the bailiff assists the jury with logistical matters such as meeting each morning, getting lunch and moving into deliberations.

Court Clerk — This person manages the court, including handling all the paperwork necessary for a hearing or trial, posting the court's docket and dealing with the demands of litigants and attorneys.

Court Reporter — This is a job that is changing with advances in technology. Court reporters traditionally take down or record everything said in court and prepare transcripts for later trials and appeals.

A Trial Docket Primer

Here is the scene in a typical Georgia superior court as it begins the morning session: the litigants and their witnesses for several cases on the judge's docket fill the courtroom. Outside on benches in the hallways are more divorcing people, witnesses and lawyers attempting to resolve their cases before court comes to order. The judge calls the docket and checks the status of each case with the attorneys. Those attorneys may want an opportunity to talk settlement, request a continuance or ask to speak with the judge in chambers about a particular issue that needs clarification.

The judge examines those cases ready for trial, and the oldest case usually takes precedence. If there is an emergency issue on the docket, the court might address that problem first.

If the judge is in the midst of a trial, he or she will usually proceed with that case and reschedule the others. This is how the judicial system works, and your attorney is powerless to change it. You may prepare for trial and bring your witnesses from all over only to have your case continued.

The best you can expect, in many cases, is for your lawyer to call the courthouse on the day before your case is set. Your attorney can try to determine where you are on the docket and what cases precede yours. Some court clerks will tell your lawyer if a trial is in progress or if a judge must clear a more pressing case before beginning yours. Other judges may require you, your witnesses and your lawyer to appear in court every time the case is set.

JUDGE OR JURY BEST IN PROPERTY CASES?

The Georgia legal system guarantees the right to a trial by jury, so either party to a divorce or other family matter may request a jury. If such a request is not made, a judge determines the matters at issue.

In any divorce case, jury findings regarding the characterization and valuation of property are binding, including decisions on division of property. Some cases are better tried before a jury, while others are best before the court. Situations where it may be advantageous to ask a judge to rule include:

- The case is strong on the facts, as juror emotions may weaken strong facts.
- There are time or monetary limitations, as it takes longer for a case to come up for jury trial than for a bench trial, and it takes longer to prepare for a jury trial and try a case before a jury.
- The judge who presides over the trial has ruled in your favor at hearings for temporary relief or other preliminary matters.

Situations where you might be better off with a jury include when:

- Your case is strong on the law. Jurors tend to see the law in absolutes, while a judge may find limitations.
- You are the petitioner, since you present evidence first and are in the best position to make a good first impression on the jury.
- You want to preserve a strong case for appeal, since there is more chance for error in a case tried by a jury.
- The judge who will hear your case has a history of rulings adverse to litigants in your position or antipathy to your attorney.

Keep Composed on the Stand

If your case moves through the system until you are actually called to testify, focus on the issue at hand. Sit up straight in your seat, speak clearly and be polite. Remember the finder of fact (judge or jury) evaluates your responses and your overall demeanor. While on the witness stand, do not argue with the other lawyer or answer questions in a haughty or sarcastic fashion.

Think of the opposing counsel as a master interrogator. Do not try to be clever. If you feel you are facing an attack, do not strike back. The other side may try to get you upset and alter your focus. Do not help them achieve their goal.

When the other side questions you, give truthful and accurate answers. Lying on the stand is unethical, illegal and impractical. All it takes to ruin your credibility with the trial judge is to be caught lying on the stand, even about some insignificant fact.

Offering more information than the other lawyer requests can prove the other side's case. Once you answer the question as briefly as possible, don't say another word. If you are concerned about how to answer certain questions, discuss this with your lawyer.

Your lawyer should detail a specific plan for handling the case at trial, based on the information available and what he knows about the judge. You may think a fact or piece of evidence is absolutely essential, but it could annoy the judge and throw your lawyer off stride.

Most divorce lawyers want to know how you will testify. Your refusal to follow your lawyer's advice may cause you to lose your case.

BASIC RULES FOR GIVING TESTIMONY

Always tell the truth.

Listen to the question.

Make certain you understand the question asked.

Be sure to answer the question.

Take your time.

Answer only the question asked.

Make your answer audible and distinct.

Do not guess about what is being asked.

Avoid boxing yourself in.

Don't argue with the opposing counsel.

If you forget the question, ask the attorney to repeat it.

Dress appropriately.

It is okay for witnesses or your attorney to have spoken to you but not to coach you.

Do not respond to the question until the opposing attorney completes the question and is silent.

24

A Divorce Is Granted

If the divorce has been agreed to and the parties sign a final decree, only one side and his or her attorney are required to appear in court to prove up the divorce, although you can decide if attending the final hearing might be psychologically good for you.

Some people may find it helpful to conclude the divorce with this formality, a bookend to the ritual of marriage. Also, consider discussing with a counselor the near future, when you might cope with the grief of ending the marriage and the many details of the divorce.

THE FINAL DECREE

When your divorce is final, the judge signs a document called the final decree of divorce. This document ends the marriage and spells out the terms of the divorce. If the dissolution takes place through a settlement, the final decree of divorce usually contains a settlement agreement signed by the parties and the judge that makes it binding. If the case is resolved in trial, the decree spells out the court's ruling or the jury verdict.

As part of the process, your attorney should review the decree and any settlement agreement with you before the divorce is final. Make certain you understand the requirements, because violating the agreement can bring a contempt citation.

Emotions normally run high during a trial or settlement talks, so people may forget certain issues such as the exact distribution of proceeds from the sale of the marital residence or who gets which music CDs. Put your copy of the divorce papers in a handy place, since you may need to refer to them in the future as disputes or questions arise.

DETAILS, DETAILS, DETAILS...

Once your divorce is final, either by agreement or in a trial before a judge or jury, you have items to follow up on and tasks to complete. The most important of these include:

- If you plan to appeal, there are strict time limits, so discuss these with your attorney immediately.
- Change your will, medical directive and power of attorney.
- Prepare and file real estate deeds transferring property interests.
- Transfer titles or bills of sale to automobiles, boats or other property.
- Enter a Qualified Domestic Relations Order (QDRO) to divide a retirement account.
- Prepare and file insurance forms with change of beneficiary.
- Make sure you have health insurance.

- For women, request a name change with the correct governmental entity and creditors. (NOTE: The name change should be ordered in the final decree.)
- Inform creditors and others of an address change as well as a name change.
- Change name and address on bank accounts.
- File IRS Form 8332 to establish dependency exemptions.
- If applicable, file income withholding orders for child support collection.

STILL UNHAPPY? TRY AN APPEAL

You might expect half of all divorcing people to feel they were treated badly in the divorce. But one study of attitudes following divorce indicates that as many as 80% of litigants feel they were taken to the cleaners. That's an overwhelming percentage, and it tells an interesting story. Apparently, both sides in many divorces come away with a bad taste in their mouths.

If you feel cheated, you have 30 days to file an appeal of the divorce decree, and you should act sooner rather than later.

A motion for a new trial rarely succeeds unless the court failed to consider a material fact in evidence or the court made an error in its ruling. Remember, the judge considering this motion is the same one who heard your entire case. A motion for a new trial is asking the judge to admit that he or she made a mistake serious enough to warrant correction. The judge is not likely to admit such a mistake without clear and convincing evidence.

If your motion fails, consider an appeal to a higher court. Either party to a divorce has the right to appeal the final decree, although most appeals fail. In divorce cases, most successful appeals deal with such issues as the trial judge not allowing a key witness to testify or some other mistake of law.

If you reach this point, you and your attorney should evaluate your chances of a successful appeal versus the tremendous cost in time and money. With each appeal, you have to pay for a copy of the court file (clerk's record) and a copy of the trial transcript (reporter's record), in addition to paying your lawyer to write a history of the case. If you hire a lawyer who specializes in appeals, that lawyer has to spend many hours becoming familiar with the facts of the case before writing the appeal brief. If the appeal is not successful, the lawyer may have to draft other documents and briefs for the Georgia Supreme Court, and that means additional expense.

Seeking redress through the appeals process is possible, but it is much more expensive and difficult than having a trial free from legal errors.

S N A P S H O T

RELOCATION, A NATIONAL HOT-BUTTON ISSUE

His View

He was devastated by divorce. He hated not seeing his son every day. She didn't understand how much he enjoyed rough-housing on the lawn or reading bedtime stories.

Since they signed the divorce decree, she complained about everything. He couldn't be a day late on his child support payments or a minute late after a weekend visit. She criticized the way their son looked following those weekends. Before they divorced, she told everyone what a good, active father he was. Now he was suddenly the world's worst.

To heck with her, he thought. He looked forward to his son's weekend visits, carefully planning their activities and making sure the fridge was stocked with his favorite food. Those weekends were always great. It gave them a chance to reconnect.

When he told her that he would like to see his son more during the week, she pulled out the divorce papers and told him he should have thought of that before he signed. He regretted not asking for more time, but he never thought she would be so rigid.

Then she started seeing someone new. The relationship moved fast and within six months, they married. Her new husband was okay, but another man was spending more time with his son than he was. Those weekend visits seemed even more important. He didn't want this new man taking his only son away.

So he met with his lawyer to ask questions about requesting the court to modify the child custody agreements. He wanted more visitation and felt he had a good case.

His son told him over and over that he wanted to spend more time with him. He was a good father who gave the mother extra money when she asked him to pay for swim lessons and other extracurriculars.

Before he could file papers for the modification, though, she had a surprise for him. He could not believe what he was reading. She notified him that in 60 days, she and his son were moving 1,400 miles away. In the divorce decree, she had the right to designate the primary residence without regard to geographic location. Her new husband took a better job offer in the Mountain West and they would join him there.

He was outraged. He immediately contacted his attorney and let her know that he was going to fight the move. She had to suspect he wouldn't give in that easily.

Her View

She knew the divorce was hard on everyone. She tried to move past the anger and hurt feelings for the sake of their son. But all the little things she hated about her ex when they were married seemed amplified after the divorce.

She hated the way he gave their son everything he wanted. When the boy went to visit his father, he had no rules, ate junk food and never went to bed at a decent time. That meant for a week after one of his father-son weekends, her son had to be retrained on the rules of her house. The transition was never smooth.

Even when they were married, she was always the heavy. Now she didn't control anything. He was always late returning their son on Sunday evenings. When she asked him to make sure the boy bathed over the weekend, he would shrug his shoulders and say, "He's a boy. He's going to get dirty, play hard and hate baths. Who am I to take that away from him?" He didn't have a clue what it was like to be a real parent and enforce rules on their son.

She also felt her ex was instigating war, begging for more visitation. It was already stressful for their son to visit every other weekend. Increasing the overnight visits with him would ruin their son's routine.

She didn't expect to meet someone and fall in love so quickly. But her new husband was wonderful. He got along with her son and was a good role model.

Shortly after she remarried, the boy's father began to pester her for more visitation. She could tell he was uncomfortable with another man spending so much time with their son. She asked him to give her new husband a chance, explaining that he was a really good man. Instead of being reassured, he became even more insecure.

When her new husband got the job offer that would double his salary, they made the difficult decision to relocate to Denver, Colorado. It wasn't an easy choice, but with the increase in his salary they could afford private school for the boy and she would not have to work so hard. She knew her ex would not be happy. But they had valid reasons for the move that would benefit their son. And since the domicile of her son was not restricted in the divorce decree, they were going.

With the decision made, she instructed her attorney to draft the notice letter. She hoped for a compromise.

The Result

The resulting court battle was costlier and more contentious than their divorce. He felt the move would rob him of his son. He asked for more visitation time when she was doing the exact opposite.

She could see nothing but the positive attributes of this move. The higher income would greatly benefit their son by providing him with a more comfortable and privileged life. She agreed to let their son stay with him in Atlanta over much of the summer and share school breaks.

In the end, they relocated. In addition to allowing him increased visitation during the summer, she was ordered to pay the cost of all transportation for their son's trips from Denver to Atlanta.

25

Relocating a Child and Other Modifications

The final divorce decree is a living, breathing document, especially if the couple has children or if payments must be made from one ex to the other in the future.

Both people often spend months after the divorce determining how flexible to be with its provisions as lives change and children get older. Only the two parents can decide if they will treat the decree literally or use it merely as a guideline.

Changes happen in every family. Must you panic at every proposed change, or are you ready to go with the flow? When these changes come up, each side must ask themselves the following questions:

- Will this change cost me money and create a hardship?
- Is this change better for the children and for myself?

- Will the change be short or long term?
- Although I may be okay with this change, will it lay the groundwork for a change down the road that I don't want?
- Do we both understand the limitations of this change?
- Must we put this change in writing, or should we keep it verbal?
- Can I trust my ex to do this unofficially, or should I have my attorney "paper" it?

Major life changes often bring efforts to legally modify a divorce decree as it relates to the children. The most common modifications involve child custody, support and visitation. Many modification agreements are made by the parties, without court approval. But if one parent later reneges on the agreement, it may not be enforceable. If there is any residual friction between parents, it's best to obtain a court order before relying on agreements.

RELOCATING A CHILD

A frequently contentious type of modification is an attempt to relocate children from one city or state to another. Relocation is often a contested issue in a divorce, but it arises more commonly in modification actions when one parent seeks to move the children away from the area where the other parent lives. The shift toward joint custody has led to an increased occurrence of residence restrictions. Many states, including Georgia, struggle with the relocation issue.

At odds are two legal rights. On the one hand, any person in this country has a constitutional right to mobility. We allow people to move freely from one place to another with no restrictions. But what about the right of children to have access to both parents? A problem arises when the parent with primary possession of the children attempts to relocate them far enough away from the other parent to make visitation and a continuing relationship between the children and the other parent difficult. Does the moving parent have the right to take the children or is it in the best interest of the children for them to stay near the non-moving parent? These relocations not only cause emotional upheavals, but they can create financial difficulties, too. Here are two examples:

The divorced mother of three children meets a man and falls in love. He is the heir to a family business in another state. The children's father pays some child support and spends a great deal of time with his kids. The boyfriend asks the woman to marry him and move to his city with her children. What right is most important here?

A man with sole custody of his young daughter gets an ultimatum from his employer: accept a transfer to another city or find another job. The mother is established in the community, where she also grew up, and the children are part of her extended family. What should the father do?

"Relocation is one of the really hot topics," says Dr. Elizabeth King of the Peachtree Psychological Association in Atlanta. "More and more people are litigating and writing about the issue of relocation, but it's impossible to come up with clear guidelines because a relocation can occur in many instances."

Any relocation creates stress on the children. The key is looking at how settled the children are in the community, and are they old enough to maintain a relationship with the parent left behind, says Dr. King, who often offers expert testimony in court on such cases. If a parent has maintained a loving relationship, though, a court may find it hard to approve a move.

Dr. King says she worked on one case in which a parent was offered a new job with a bump in pay exceeding $100,000, and the judge ruled the children must stay behind with the other parent.

"It's a nightmare," Dr. King says of the decisions the courts and parents face. Exacerbating the issue is the move away from parents maintaining sole custody in favor of joint custody arrangements giving each parent the legal right to the children.

"For the really decent people who have been involved with their children, how do they make these choices?" Dr. King asks.

Few Georgia cases have discussed the relocation issue in depth. In *Bodne* v. *Bodne*, however, The Georgia Supreme Court found that relocation by a parent out of state with the child can affect the welfare of the child and might justify modification of a prior custody order.

The case recognized that the trial court must consider the best interest of the child, even if a move might substantially improve the life of the parent. Clearly, it is now more difficult for a parent to relocate their children to another jurisdiction, particularly in cases which involve significant post-divorce co-parenting.

CHANGE OF CUSTODY

Relocation is an example of a change in circumstances that could result in a request for a change in custody of the children. A full-blown custody trial is the most extreme example of an attempted modification. The parent asking for a change must show that the modification would be in the best interest of the child. He or she must also show that the circumstances of the child or one of the parents has materially and substantially changed since the current agreement was made or a court order issued. You should think long and hard about the effect of any return to the court system. Is this action necessary for the child, or are you just upset? Are there other ways to accomplish what you want? And will the positive effect of the modification offset the negative effect of bringing the action?

Just consider the expense. Suing for custody can be one of the most expensive legal moves you can make. The money you spend in attorney's fees, expert witnesses and probably lost income during that time—not to mention the lost sleep and increased anxiety—might purchase a very nice education for your children.

MORE OR LESS CHILD SUPPORT

If the income of either spouse increases or decreases significantly, the amount of child support may be adjusted. Look at the overall financial situation before going to court and forcing your ex to pay more support. If he or she spends money on the children above and beyond child support, could those expenditures be endangered if you play hardball in court?

Ask your lawyer to assist you in calculating the projected new child support payments under your facts. You can determine if those extra payments equal or exceed the amount you would get if you took the matter back to court.

Sometimes, parents obligated to pay child support take defensive actions when called upon to pay more. Increasing child support is another reason some parents seek custody. These actions often fail, but they create additional expense for the custodial parent seeking increased child support.

The fear of a custody battle is amplified if a parent has had less than exemplary conduct since the divorce. Living with a friend of the opposite sex may not cause you to lose your children, but it can muddy the waters.

MODIFYING VISITATION

Children get older and circumstances change. A noncustodial parent may want more visitation, or the children may become teenagers and want to spend more time with their friends instead of going to a parent's house. A child may want to spend an entire summer backpacking with an uncle across Europe.

Modifications are expensive if you have to go to court. You might spend thousands of dollars for an extra evening of visitation or to deny your ex that amount of time with the children.

26

Getting On with Your Life

How many of us know divorced people who simply can't let go of a lost love? It's a natural human quality, but is it healthy?

It has been said that people don't go to divorce court for justice. At the most, what they can expect is a conclusion. The very nature of divorce may make it impossible to bring fairness into an emotionally destructive process. People may spend years angry with a former spouse and bitter over unchangeable facts. While a certain amount of emotion and anger is justified, don't ruin the rest of your life worrying about the behavior of others. When a door closes, a window opens. Looking for an open window is more productive than spending time banging against a closed door. Some therapists and counselors actually practice marriage disengagement therapy, helping people move out of a marriage so they can go forward into the future.

You have to look at the big picture and see your life over the long haul. Sure, you might upset your children when you tell them about the divorce, and they may remain upset for a time after. But studies show that after the first six months, kids generally rebound and do even better than prior to the divorce, when tensions in the home were often strained.

WHEN CONFRONTED, CHOOSE REASON

The happiest people after a divorce are those who feel generous enough to be fair with the person who once inspired them to hate and dread. The idea that you must never back down, allow no compromise and stick to your guns does nothing for you in the family court system and very little in life.

If you can afford to be generous with your ex (and especially your children), do it. Here's an example:

A man with two children agreed to pay $1,200 a month in child support after the divorce. As time went along, he also picked up the cost of music lessons and tuition to a music camp for his kids, and worked with his ex to establish college funds for both children. He was not obligated to do all this, except for the obligation any good parent would feel.

When the man asked to extend his weekend visitation so he could take the children with him and his new wife to their lake cabin on Sunday, at first the children's mother refused. She still felt he disappointed her, but the sincerity of his commitment to the children was so strong that she couldn't deny him. He was reasonable and responsible, and she came to the conclusion that she should relent.

Reason and generosity often trump toughness at this point. Your children will respect you for your restraint and it may even make your ex easier to deal with over the long haul.

But When Reason Doesn't Work...

One person who simply won't play by the rules, however, could bring on the necessity for an enforcement action. These actions are used to enforce the payment of child support and attorney's fees, compel child custody or visitation orders and control certain types of financial and property matters.

Contempt of court is one remedy of an enforcement action. The standard for contempt is fairly understandable. One person must willfully refuse to comply with a clear, specific order of the court central to the obligation in question.

For example, the paying spouse may fail to send child support or maintenance payments, even though he or she has worked and instead has chosen to spend the money on other things. Most likely this is contempt.

A contempt action can lead to jail, a fine or both for failure to comply with the divorce decree. Sometimes an action like this is necessary to convince the offending person that this is serious business and he or she should straighten up and fly right or something very distasteful will happen.

Under a contempt action, you or your ex may be placed in jail and can only be released by purging the conduct in question. For example, the court may order you to jail until all or most of the back payments are made. If you are truly unable to pay, the court may not keep you in jail. But you'd be surprised how often relatives or close friends come forward with the cash to pay the amount due.

For many people, these support payments are essential to the maintenance of an ongoing household. Don't let the paying spouse slide on something that seems to be a one-time occurrence. Sometimes people make threats to withhold support payments, and you should take those threats seriously. If the party begins to act contemptuously toward you, keep detailed records of unmet obligations.

Once your ex misses a payment or two, don't wait too long to file a contempt action. Some of the most patient people wait until they are owed tens of thousands of dollars before making a move. In cases like these, you may have to accept installment payments to pay off the large debt.

Your relationship with the ex is directly related to your initial actions after the divorce. If you file a contempt action immediately after he or she fails to comply, this will send a signal that you will punish non-compliance. You need to establish that you will not tolerate missed support payments or a failure to comply with the financial arrangements either agreed to or ordered by the court.

You will be accused of being inflexible, but just remind your ex that those you owe money to are even less flexible. By being steadfast, you may modify future behavior.

27

Prenups and Postnups: Anticipating Another Marriage

People with large assets are often wary about marriage, fearing a potential spouse might want a large property settlement more than a long and loving marital relationship. A premarital agreement, or "prenup," offers one way to make that big financial decision and still feel protected.

Historically, extremely well-to-do people use prenups to protect themselves from gold diggers and charlatans. With growth in the available pool of wealthy people, prenups gain favor with a wider group of people whose minds are eased by these protective agreements.

A prenup is simply a premarital contract confirming or modifying the characterization of property. Both parties must agree to and sign the contract. It is common for premarital agreements to confirm that certain assets brought into the marriage by one party remain that party's separate property.

238

The property addressed in the prenup may be an interest in real or personal property, retirement benefits, stock options and leasehold interests. A prenup may also provide that a spouse's income and earnings are that spouse's separate property.

People of modest means also increasingly use prenups. A person with a job and few liquid assets might execute a premarital agreement to protect his or her retirement account or future earnings in case of divorce, separation or death.

In fact, the internet offers an inexpensive, simple solution for many people. It's possible to find one of a variety of Web sites offering templates for prenuptial agreements. If the finances are straightforward, this is a good option for many people, providing a basic document to set forth your intentions.

It's surprising the number of people willing to enter a marriage unwilling to disclose finances to their soon-to-be spouse, one reason a prenuptial agreement might fail. Full disclosure is necessary, allowing both people to know about all assets and debts. If you or the person you plan to marry are unwilling to share these details, think carefully about the possible motives and ramifications. Remember, money is the number one cause of marital disputes.

Prenups tend to simplify potentially complicated and messy financial situations. For instance, some assets are not easily divisible, such as an interest in a family-owned business or a large tract of real estate.

If one spouse owns a portion of that hard-to-divide property as his or her separate property, a premarital agreement could keep the entire asset from being divided or sold.

Consider two situations that might warrant a prenup. If you have significant assets but your spouse does not, this represents the stereotype for a prenup. Or possibly you have wealth and children but you marry someone with children and few accumulated assets. Would you wish to risk leaving accumulated wealth to your new stepchildren?

Prenuptial Agreement Protects Assets

The following matters may be addressed in a prenup:

- The rights and obligations to property by either party.
- The right to buy, sell, use, transfer, exchange, abandon, lease, consume, assign, create a security interest in, mortgage, encumber, dispose of or otherwise manage and control property.
- The disposition of property on separation, marital dissolution or death.
- The modification or elimination of spousal support.
- The making of a will, trust or other arrangement to carry out the provisions of the agreement.
- Ownership of a life insurance policy.
- Choice of law governing the agreement.
- Any personal matter not in violation of public policy or criminal statutes.
- Providing income from all separate property to remain separate property, precluding creation of any marital property during marriage and partitioning future earnings.

You cannot, however, expect a prenuptial agreement to adversely affect the right of a child to support in the event of divorce. In some cases, the party who requested the prenup may decide after the marriage to amend or soften the terms of the agreement. Any change in a prenup at this time must be done by written agreement signed by both people.

Why Have a Postnuptial Agreement?

Postnups are much like prenups in the way they deal with assets, except that they are executed *after* the marriage. Like premarital agreements, postnups must be in writing and signed.

The agreement should specify any actual partition or exchange of property. Through the use of a postnup, spouses may convert marital property or their separate property into the other spouse's separate property. In the event of a divorce, the property is already divided.

How to Enforce or Break These Agreements

Prenuptial or postnuptial agreements are tougher to break than they were just a few years ago, when judges were allowed nearly unlimited discretion to decide their fairness. Now, a signed prenuptial agreement will likely hold if both people fully disclose all assets before the agreement. If someone tries to hide assets, the judge will likely invalidate the agreement.

A court usually evaluates three areas to determine validity of such agreements:

- Was the agreement obtained through fraud, duress, or mistake, or through misrepresentation or nondisclosures of material fact?
- Was the agreement unconscionable?
- Have the facts and circumstances changed since the agreement was executed so as to make enforcement unfair or unreasonable?

A case decided in 2006, *Corbett* v. *Corbett*, illustrates the approach Georgia courts take. A couple married in 1987 after signing a prenuptial agreement, which said in part that each person would retain separate property and assets as well as waive the possibility of alimony.

When the wife filed for divorce in 2002, the husband sought to enforce the agreement. A trial determined that the wife neither read the agreement before signing nor had an attorney review the document. Also, the wife did not provide the husband with

241

a list of personal property or an estimate of their value. She also had no knowledge of the man's income.

When the trial court ruled in the wife's favor, an appeal went to the state supreme court, which also decided against the man. The failure to disclose details of the man's income was deemed critical to the woman's decision to waive alimony in the prenuptial agreement.

This was an instance when the failure to disclose everything prior to marriage invalidated the efforts to secure a prenuptial agreement.

28

The End of Ignorance

Once you are divorced, you are free to fall in love, get married or place your trust in people again. You are entitled to happiness, and happiness usually involves love. If you want it, you should pursue it.

But there are things you should not ever do again. You should not stay ignorant of the financial details of your family, the money foibles of your loved one or how to protect your assets in the event of another divorce.

What you should do is the following:

- Consider some kind of premarital agreement that simply spells out financial rules between you.
- Always be the documented spouse who keeps financial records at your fingertips.
- Thoroughly review income tax forms, contracts and other financial instruments before signing them.

- During the marriage, periodically examine reports from the three major credit bureaus to know how many accounts you have and how your household income is used.
- If you are unfortunate enough to face another divorce, learn from your experience.
- You should know how to divide marital assets more productively.
- If you are owed some kind of support payments over time, require life insurance on the paying spouse.
- You should know how to best handle disposition of the marital residence, retirement plans and deferred compensation programs such as stock options.
- You should remember that child support is ordered in almost every case, and you can use state guidelines to estimate child support.

Never again will you be in the dark about your financial standing, and that's a good thing whether you get a divorce tomorrow or live with the same person the rest of your life.

APPENDIX A

Professionals List

The following is a compilation of Georgia profession-als who deal with family law issues on a regular basis as part of their practices. The individuals are included here because of their professional credentials, outstand-ing reputations, and long experience. Still, their inclu-sion here does not constitute an endorsement of their work by the author or the publisher.

If you are in need of the services of anyone included on this list, we recommend that you interview more than one service provider and make your own determination as to their fitness for the tasks you have for them.

CERTIFIED PUBLIC ACCOUNTANTS

David Deeter
Frazier & Deeter
600 Peachtree Street, NE
Suite 1900
Atlanta 30308
(404) 253-7500

Lyn Reagan
Bennett, Thrasher & Co.
3330 Cumberland Blvd, Suite 100
Atlanta 30339
(770) 396-2200

Steve Byrne
Mauldin & Jenkins, CPA
200 Galleria Pkwy, SE
Suite 1700
Atlanta 30339
(770) 541-5425

Scott Thurman
Thurman Financial
Consulting, Inc.
10892 Crabapple Rd, Suite 300
Roswell 30075
(678) 323-3473

Bruce McEwen
Moore Stephens Tiller
780 Johnson Ferry Rd, Suite 325
Atlanta 30342
(404) 256-1606

Laurie G. Dyke
Investigative Accounting Group
1842 Bishops Green Drive
Marietta 30062
(770) 565-3098

HLM Financial Group
Two Decatur Town Center
Suite 150
125 Clairemont Avenue
Decatur 30030
(404) 836-1120

Charles Johnson
Robinson, Grimes & Co, P.C.
P.O. Box 4299
Columbus 31904
(706) 324-5435

John D. Houser
Miller, Ray & Houser
99 West Paces Ferry Rd, NW
Atlanta 30305
(404) 365-1460

Stanley M. Smith
Carr, Riggs & Ingram LLC
4360 Chamblee-Dunwoody Rd
Suite 420
Atlanta 30341
(770) 457-6606

Ronald A. Swichkow
519 Johnson Ferry Rd, NE
Building A, Suite 100
Marietta 30068
(404) 231-3500

Stephen M. Berman
3475 Lenox Rd, NE, Suite 950
Atlanta 30326
(404) 262-2181

Joseph B. Smith
Smith & Howard, P.C.
171 17th Street, NW, Suite 900
Atlanta 30363
(404) 874-6244

Robert Arogeti
Habif, Arogeti & Wynne, LLP
5565 Glenridge Connector
Suite 200
Atlanta 30342
(404) 892-9651

FINANCIAL PLANNING ADVISORS

N. B. (Bud) Murphy
Citigroup Family Office
3333 Peachtree Rd, NE, Suite 800
Atlanta 30326
(404) 266-6313
(800) 688-6002 ext. 6313

George Beylouni
Bey-Douglas
1640 Powers Ferry Rd, Suite 100
Marietta 30067
(770) 858-0001

M. Ann Cox
Mellon Private Wealth
The Forum, Suite 950
3290 Northside Parkway, N.W.
Atlanta 30327
(678) 538-2000

Donna Barwick
Mellon Private Wealth
The Forum, Suite 950
3290 Northside Parkway, N.W.
Atlanta 30327
(678) 538-2000

D. Jack Sawyer
Mellon Private Wealth
The Forum, Suite 950
3290 Northside Parkway, N.W.

Atlanta 30327
(678) 538-2000

Hunter Groton
Mellon Private Wealth
The Forum, Suite 950
3290 Northside Parkway, N.W.
Atlanta 30327
(678) 538-2000

David Bokman
Asset Management Advisors
4401 Northside Pkwy, NW
Suite 120
Atlanta 30327-3065
(404) 419-3260

Wes French
French Wolf & Farr
3445 Peachtree Rd, Suite 575
Atlanta 30326
(404) 604-3400

Andrew (Andy) J. Berg
Homrich & Berg, Inc.
3060 Peachtree Rd, Suite 830
Atlanta 30305
(404) 264-1400

John G. McColskey
Homrich & Berg, Inc.
3060 Peachtree Rd, Suite 830
Atlanta 30305
(404) 264-1400

Marcia M. Murray
Homrich & Berg, Inc.
3060 Peachtree Rd, Suite 830
Atlanta 30305
(404) 264-1400

Frances G. Rogers
Checks & Balances, Inc.
3290 Northside Parkway
Suite 375
Atlanta 30327
(404) 233-0560

Michael E. Stogner, VP
Bank of America, NA,
Private Client Group
600 Peachtree St, NE
Suite 1100
Atlanta, Georgia 30308
(404) 607-6219

Michael J. Wagner, CFP
Merrill Lynch
3455 Peachtree Rd, NE
Suite 1000
Atlanta 30326
(404) 264-3600

ESTATE LITIGATION

Hon. Floyd E. Propst, III
Caldwell & Watson
Atlanta
(404) 843-1956

Jack N. Sibley
Hawkins & Parnell, LLP
4000 SunTrust Plaza
303 Peachtree Street, N.E.
Atlanta 30308-3243
(404) 614-7551

ESTATE PLANNING

Joel Steven Arogeti
Kitchens Kelley Gaynes, P.C.
3495 Piedmont Rd, NE

Suite 900
Atlanta 30305
(404) 237-4100

Donna Barwick
Mellon
Atlanta
(404) 231-2340

Henry L. Bowden, Jr.
The Bowden Law Firm, P.C.
191 Peachtree St, N.E.
Suite 849
Atlanta 30303
(404) 523-8337

Stephanie B. Casteel
King & Spalding LLP
1180 Peachtree St, N.E.
Atlanta 30309
(404) 572-3577

A. Kimbrough Davis
Kilpatrick Stockton LLP
1100 Peachtree St, Suite 2800
Atlanta 30309-4530
(404) 815-6655

Douglas W. Duncan
Lefkoff, Duncan, Grimes, Miller
& McSwain, P.C.
Suite 806, 11 Piedmont Ctr
3495 Piedmont Rd, N.E.
Atlanta, 30305-1758
(404) 262-2000

Robert G. Edge
Alston & Bird, LLP
1201 W. Peachtree St.
Atlanta 30309
(404) 881-7470

David F. Golden
Troutman Sanders, LLP
600 Peachtree St. N.E.
Suite 5200
Atlanta
(404) 885-3344

Milford B. Hatcher, Jr.
Jones Day
1420 Peachtree St. N.E.
Suite 800
Atlanta
(404) 521-3939

Zoe M. Hicks
Hicks & Hicks
2296 Henderson Mill Rd
Suite 110
Atlanta 30345-2739
(770) 493-7775

Clifford G. Hoffman
1532 Dunwoody Villiage
Parkway, Suite 205
Atlanta 30338
(678) 935-3500

Charles D. Hurt, Jr.
Sutherland Asbill & Brennan, LLP
999 Peachtree St., Suite 2300
Atlanta 30309
(404) 853-8143

John Raymond Jones, Jr.
King & Spalding LLP
1180 Peachtree St, N.W.
14th floor
Atlanta 30309
(404) 572-3537
(404) 572-5130

James R. Kanner
Nelson Mullins Riley & Scarborough, LLP
999 Peachtree St, Suite 1400
Atlanta, GA 30309
(404) 817-6162

William J. Linkous, Jr.
Powell Goldstein, LLP
1201 W. Peachtree St. N.W.
14th floor
Atlanta 30309
(404) 572-6600

Frank S. McGaughey, III
Powell Goldstein, LLP
1201 Peachtree St. N.W.
14th floor
Atlanta 30309
(404) 572-6651

Dora A. Miller
Lefkoff, Duncan, Grimes
& Miller
10 Piedmont Center NE
Suite 806
Atlanta 30305-1737
(404) 262-2000

Hubert Duncan Moseley, III
191 Peachtree St, NE
Suite 849
Atlanta 30303-1747
(404) 219-5916

Mary F. Radford
Georgia State University
College of Law
P.O. Box 4049
Atlanta 30302-4049
(404) 651-2088

Christopher A. Rascoe
Hendrick & Rascoe, LLC
The Rinaldi, Suite 250
3282 Northside Parkway, NW
Atlanta 30327
(404) 237-7879

E. Lowry Reid, Jr.
Page, Scrantom, Sprouse,
Tucker, & Ford, P.C.
Synovus Centre
1111 Bay Ave, 3rd Floor
Columbus 31901
(706) 324-0251

Alan F. Rothschild, Jr.
Hatcher Stubbs Land Hollis &
Rothschild, LLP
233 12th St., Suite 500
Columbus 31901
(706) 324-0201

Michael W. Rushing
Merritt & Tenney
200 Galleria Parkway
Suite 50
Atlanta 30339
(770) 952-6550

John C. Sawyer
Alston & Bird, LLP
1201 W. Peachtree St
Atlanta 30309
(404) 881-7886

John M. Sheftall
Hatcher Stubbs Land Hollis
233 12th St
500 Corporate Center
Columbus 31901
(706) 324-0201

John Wesley Spears, Jr.
Spears & Spears, P.C.
315 W. Ponce de Leon Ave
Suite 970
Decatur 30030
(404) 377-5822

James D. Spratt, Jr.
King & Spalding LLP
1180 Peachtree St
Atlanta 30309
(404) 572-4620

J. Douglas Stewart
Stewart, Melvin &
Frost, LLP
200 Main St, Suite 600
Gainesville 30501
(770) 536-0101

Wayne R. Vason
Troutman Sanders, LLP
600 Peachtree St, NE
Suite 5200
Atlanta 30308-2216
(404) 885-3232

John A. Wallace
King & Spalding LLP
1180 Peachtree St
Atlanta 30309
(404) 572-4932

MENTAL HEALTH PROFESSIONALS

David M. Alexander
Atlanta Developmental Con.
2997 Piedmont Rd
Atlanta 30305
(404) 816-9501

Judith P Nurik
3901 Roswell Rd
Marietta 30062
(770) 509-8266

Maureen Gallagher Martin
2801 Buford Hwy NE
Atlanta 30329-2149
(404) 636-1108

Susan Wachler
1900 Century Pl Ste. 200
Atlanta 30345
(404) 325-4584

Leslie P Mackinnon
1836 Walthall Dr NW
Atlanta 30318-2647
(404) 603-5335

Ann-Marie Meehan
25-B Lenox Pointe, NE
Atlanta, GA 30324
(404)266-0962

Gloria DeSantis Meaux, PhD
18-B Lenox Pointe, NE
Atlanta 30324
(404) 841-9293

Mark Vakkur, MD
2200 Century Parkway
Suite 200
Atlanta 30345
(404) 964-9883

Michael Banov, MD
11755 Pointe Place, Suite A-1
Alpharetta 30076
(770) 667-1264

Roy Sanders, MD
The Marcus Institute
1920 Briarcliff Rd
Atlanta 30329
(404) 419-4000

H. Elizabeth King, Ph.D.
Peachtree Psychological
Associates
2045 Peachtree St
Suite 150
Atlanta 30309
(404) 352-4348

REALTORS

Glennis Beacham
Beacham & Company
The Forum
3290 Northside Parkway
Suite 100
Atlanta 30327
(404) 261-6300

Jay Letts
Maple Realty Inc
311 Buckhead Ave NE
Atlanta 30305-2305
(404) 233-2747

Holly Eittreim
Century 21 / Dwellings
1640 Piedmont Rd
Atlanta 30324
(678) 488-8080

Mark Chernesky
Coldwell Banker
(404) 262-1234

BANKERS

Gary Gallman
Wachovia Securities
1742 Mt. Vernon Rd
Suite 200
Dunwoody 30338
(404) 822-6004

Nandy Hurst
SunTrust Bank
P.O. Box 4418
Atlanta 30302
(404) 724-3418

Beth Heavern, Senior Vice
President & Branch Manager
Georgia Commerce Bank
3625 Cumberland Blvd
Building Two
Atlanta 30339
(678) 631-1240

Ann C. Lichtefeld
Community Bank of the South
3324 Canton Rd
Marietta, GA 30056
(678) 594-7310

Shellee B. Spagnoletto, CFP
Vice President Private
Banking
Northern Trust Bank
3282 Northside Parkway, NW
Suite 100
Atlanta 30327
(404) 279-5200

MORTGAGE BROKERS

Janice Phillips

Community Bank of the South
3016 Atlanta Rd
Smyrna 30080
(770) 436-4567

Jim Heitzer
Neighborhood Mortgage, Inc.
1835 Lockeway Dr
Suite 306
Alpharetta 30004
(678) 990-8608

BUSINESS VALUATION EXPERTS

Meredith Damm, ASA
Fountainhead Advisors
3769 North Stratford Rd
Atlanta 30342
(404) 254-1300

David Deeter
Frazier & Deeter
600 Peachtree St, NE
Suite 1900
Atlanta 30308
(404) 253-7500

Lyn Reagan
Bennett, Thrasher & Co.
3625 Cumberland Blvd.
Suite 1000
Atlanta 30339
(770) 396-2200

Scott Thurman
Thurman Financial
Consulting, Inc.
10892 Crabapple Rd, Suite 300
Roswell 30075
(678) 323-3473

Shawn Fowler
Frazier & Deeter
600 Peachtree St, NE, Suite 1900
Atlanta 30308
(404) 253-7500

Sherri Holder
FairShare Financial, Inc.
One Glenlake Parkway, Suite 700
Atlanta 30328
(678) 578-2570

FORENSIC CPAs

David Deeter
Frazier & Deeter
600 Peachtree St, NE, Suite 1900
Atlanta 30308
(404) 253-7500

Lyn Reagan
Bennett, Thrasher & Co.
3330 Cumberland Blvd
Suite 1000
Atlanta 30339
(770) 396-2200

Steve Byrne
Mauldin & Jenkins, CPA
200 Galleria Pkwy, SE, Suite 1700
Atlanta 30339
(770) 541-5425

Scott Thurman
Thurman Financial
Consulting, Inc.
10892 Crabapple Rd, Suite 300
Roswell 30075
(678) 323-3473

BANKRUPTCY ATTORNEYS

Richard B. Herzog Jr.
Nelson Mullins Riley
& Scarborough LLP
999 Peachtree St, N.E.
Suite 1400
Atlanta 30309-4422
(404) 817-6000

Robert B. Campos, Esq.
Lamberth, Cifelli, Stokes
& Stout, P.A.
East Tower, Suite 550
3343 Peachtree Rd, NE
Atlanta 30326-1022
(404) 262-7373

Gregory Donald Ellis, Esq.
Lamberth, Cifelli, Stokes
& Stout, P.A.
East Tower, Suite 550
3343 Peachtree Rd, N.E.
Atlanta 30326-1022
(404) 262-7373

Jonathon Melnick
1720 Peachtree St
Suite 214
Atlanta 30309-2449
(404) 249-8383

Keith Eady
Keith Eady & Associates, LLC
2785B Clairmont Rd, NE
Suite 105
Atlanta 30329
(404) 633-1997

INSURANCE PROFESSIONALS

Kirk Wimberly
400 Interstate North Pkwy
Atlanta 30303
(770) 612-4637

Bill Cook
State Farm
34 Peachtree St, Suite 700
Atlanta 30303
(404) 524-4986

Franklin McKinney
McKinney & Co.
P.O. Box 7
Tucker 30085
(770) 723-9901

Lloyd Patience
690 Highland Oaks Lane
Mableton 30126
(770) 941-1487

John M.E. Saad
Regional Vice President
National Life Group
3884 Fairfax Court, SE
Atlanta 30339-4410
(404) 276-8127 office
(770) 241-6749 cell

PRIVATE INVESTIGATORS

Tim McWhirter
Automatic Global
Response, LLC
3091 Univeter Road
Canton 30115
(770) 479-0021

Thomas P. Hawkins, Jr.
Hawk Private
Investigations, Inc.
400 Galleria Parkway, Suite 1500
Atlanta 30339
(770) 951-2121

RETIREMENT/EMPLOYMENT BENEFITS ATTORNEY

Benefits Law Group
2515 Resurgens Plaza
945 East Paces Ferry Rd
Atlanta 30326
(404) 995-9505

APPRAISERS

Jay Scholfield
Atlanta
(770) 924-0606

Vernon G. Abrams
Vernon Abrams, Ltd.
2996 Grandview Ave, Suite 203
Atlanta 30305
(404) 842-0567

Phillip H. Hawkins, ISA
4291 Briarcliff Road
Atlanta 30345
(404) 320-7275

DIVORCE RESOURCE GROUPS

Visions Anew Institute
131 Shadowlawn Rd, Suite 101
Marietta 30067-4329
(770) 953-288

TAX ATTORNEYS

Jack Fishman
Park Central, Suite 950
2970 Clairmont Rd
Atlanta 30329
(404) 320 9300

Doug Wright
Holland & Knight LLP
One Atlantic Center
1201 W. Peachtree St, N.E.,
Suite 2000
Atlanta, GA 30309-3400
(404) 817-8500

COLLABORATIVE LAWYERS

Emily S. Bair
Emily S. Bair
& Associates, P.C.
6100 Lake Forrest Dr, Suite 370
Atlanta 30328
(404) 806-7330

Lauren G. Alexander
Collaborative Law Office of
Lauren G. Alexander
5500 Interstate North Pkwy
Suite 544
Atlanta 30329
(770) 818-9027

MEDIATORS

M. T. Simmons, Jr
Simmons, Warren, Szczecko & McFee
315 West Ponce de Leon Ave
Suite 850
Decatur 30030
(404) 378-1711

Hylton B. Dupree, Jr
Dupree, King & Kimbrough
P.O. Box 525
Marietta 30061
(770) 424-7171

Christopher D. Olmstead
McLain & Merritt P.C.
3445 Peachtree Rd, Suite 500
Atlanta 30326
(404) 365-4542

Susan A. Hurst
Bogart & Bogart, P.C.
6400 Powers Ferry Rd
Suite 220
Atlanta 30339
(770) 352-9470

Jeff Hamby, Esq.
Huff, Woods & Hamby
707 Whitlock Ave, SW
Suite G-5
Marietta 30066
(770) 429-1001

APPENDIX B

Glossary of Family Law Terms

-A-

ACKNOWLEDGEMENT OF SERVICE: If the respondent does not wish to be formally served with the citation in a divorce, he or she may sign an acknowledgement of service acknowledging receipt of a copy of the final divorce petition.

ACTION: A lawsuit or proceeding in a court of law.

AFFIDAVIT: A written statement under oath.

ALIMONY: Periodic payments of support provided by one spouse to the other.

ANNULMENT: The marriage is declared void, as though it never took place.

ANSWER: The written response to a complaint, petition or motion.

APPEAL: A legal action where the losing party requests that a higher court review the decision.

ASSET: Everything owned by you or your spouse, including property, cars, furniture, bank accounts, jewelry, life insurance policies, businesses and retirement plans.

-B-

BENCH TRIAL: A trial where the judge determines all issues and there is no jury.

BILLING: An accounting of hours spent on your case by the attorney, his legal assistant and others. Usually calculated monthly.

BUSINESS VALUATION: Experts are used to value businesses in a divorce context. The valuation of a closely held business or professional practice is only as good as the judgment of the appraiser and the accuracy of the information relied upon. When valuing a closely held business, it is essential to have a thorough knowledge of the measures of value, the methods of valuation and Georgia case law. The valuation of professional practices requires a clear understanding of professional goodwill, and there may be a need for adjustments to the value of a business due to its lack of marketability, the size of the interest (minority or majority) and the existence or non-existence of a covenant not to compete.

-C-

CHARACTERIZATION: The process of identifying what property is separate property and what property is marital property. The court can only divide the parties' marital property and not their separate property.

CHILD SUPPORT: Money paid from one parent to the other for the benefit of their minor children.

CLOSELY HELD BUSINESS: A business that is privately owned, such as a family business.

CLOSING ARGUMENTS: Final statements by each attorney at the end of the trial when they argue to the judge or jury the evidence and the law.

COMMINGLING ASSETS: When separate and marital funds are commingled.

COMMON LAW MARRIAGE: A common law marriage comes about when a man and woman who are free to marry agree to live together as husband and wife without a formal ceremony. As of 1996, common law marriages are no longer allowed in Georgia, although the change in law did not void existing common law marriages.

CONTEMPT: Failure to follow a court order. One side can request that the court determine that the other side is in contempt for violating a court order and punish him or her.

CONTESTED ISSUES: Any or all issues upon which the parties are unable to agree and which the judge or jury at a hearing or trial must resolve.

CONTINGENT ASSET: An asset that you may receive or get later, such as a recovery from a lawsuit or a potential cause of action against a third party.

CONTINGENT LIABILITY: A liability that you may owe later, such as payments for lawsuits against either party or a guaranty that you have signed.

CONTINUANCE: Postponement of a trial or hearing.

CORROBORATING WITNESS: A person who testifies for you and backs up your story.

COUNTER CLAIM: A written request to the court for legal action, which is filed by a respondent after being served with a divorce petition.

COURT REPORTER: The person who records the testimony and court proceedings.

CUSTODY (SOLE AND JOINT): Refers to the rights and duties that parents have with respect to their children.

-D-

DECREE: The final document that the judge signs granting the divorce. The divorce decree contains all of the agreements of the parties and orders of the court with respect to all issues in the case, including custody, possession, child support, alimony and a division of the marital estate.

DEFERRED COMPENSATION: Deferred compensation includes pensions, annuities payable in the future and other forms of deferred income.

DEPOSITION: Discovery in which an attorney asks questions of the opposing party under oath.

DIRECT EXAMINATION: Questions asked of witnesses called by the attorney asking the questions.

DISCOVERY: A way of getting information from the other side or other people. Examples are interrogatories (written questions to be answered under oath), requests to produce documents and depositions.

DISSOLUTION: The legal end of a marriage.

DOCKET: A court's calendar of cases.

-E-

ENJOINED: Prohibited by the court from doing or failing to do a specific act.

EX PARTE: Communication with the judge by only one party. In order for a judge to speak with either party, in most cases the other party must have been properly notified and have an opportunity to be heard.

EXPERT WITNESS: An expert who is qualified in a certain area may testify as to his or her opinion as to the matters in which he or she is qualified. When the spouses' testimony as to the value of certain assets is widely disparate, the court may be more likely to accept a valuation supported by expert opinion. Experts in a family law case may include psychologists, business valuation experts, real estate appraisers, forensic CPA's, and others, such as art and airplane appraisers.

-F -

FILING: Giving the court clerk your legal papers to be included in the court's file.

FORENSIC ACCOUNTANT: A person who prepares an investigation of finances or who traces assets for the purpose of discovering information in a lawsuit and offering testimony in court.

-G-

GOODWILL: There are two types of goodwill: Business goodwill (also called commercial goodwill) is the business's reputation and ability, as an institution, to attract and hold business even with a change in ownership. Personal goodwill is associated with the individual professional, not the practice or business as a whole, and therefore cannot be transferred to a buyer. Personal goodwill (also called professional goodwill) does not possess value or constitute an asset separate and apart from the person of the professional, or from the professional's ability to practice the profession. Personal goodwill is not divisible on divorce and is not to be considered in the valuation of the professional's practice.

-H-

HEARING: A legal proceeding before a judge or associate judge on a motion.

I-

INFORMAL DISCOVERY: The voluntary and informal exchange of information between the parties through their attorneys, as distinguished from formal discovery (i.e., interrogatories and requests to produce documents.

INJUNCTION: An order from a court prohibiting a person from doing something.

INTERROGATORIES: Written questions submitted to a party in a divorce for that party to answer under oath.

INVENTORY AND APPRAISEMENT: The first step in identifying a couple's assets and liabilities. List the most valuable assets and take photos if possible. Most cases require a domestic relations financial affidavit, which itemizes assets and debts.

-J-

JUDGMENT or RULING: A court's decision.

JURISDICTION: The authority of the court to hear a case.

-L-

LIABILITIES: Everything owed by you or your spouse, including mortgages, credit cards or other loans.

-M-

MARITAL DEBTS: Debts undertaken during the marriage are presumed to be marital debts; a showing that the creditor agreed to look to the separate estate of the spouse incurring the debt for satisfaction of the debt and separate funds were actually used to repay the debt, however, can rebut this presumption.

MARITAL PROPERTY: Property acquired during the marriage, other than that received by gift or inheritance, is marital property and each spouse is entitled to an equitable share as decided by a judge or jury.

MARKET VALUE: Market value is the most common measure of value. It is defined as the amount a willing buyer who desires to buy but is under no obligation to buy would pay to a willing seller who desires to sell but is under no obligation to sell.

MEDIATOR: A person trained to assist parties in reaching an agreement before going to court. Mediators do not take either party's side and do not give legal advice. They are only responsible for helping the parties reach an agreement and putting that agreement into writing. In many courts, mediation of family law cases is required before going to court.

MOTION: A request made to the court, other than a petition.

-N-

NO-FAULT DIVORCE: One party must establish that he or she refuses to live with the other spouse and that there is no hope of reconciliation to receive a no-fault divorce. Neither party must show fault or wrongdoing. In Georgia, an "irretrievably broken" marriage is one of 13 grounds for divorce.

-O-

OBJECTION: Notice to the judge by one attorney that the proceedings are objectionable for some reason and the attorney wants to bring it to the attention of the judge and request a ruling.

OBLIGEE: A person to whom money, such as child support or alimony, is owed.

OBLIGOR: A person who is ordered by the court to pay money, such as child support or alimony.

OPENING STATEMENT: A brief statement by an attorney of his client's version of the facts and position on the issues and applicable law, generally at the beginning of the trial.

ORDER: A written decision signed by a judge and filed in the case record that contains the judge's decision on some part of a case, usually on a motion.

OVERRULED: When an attorney objects to something said or done in the courtroom, this means the judge disagrees with the objecting attorney.

-P-

PARENTING COURSE: Teaches parents how to co-parent, help their children cope with divorce and other family issues. Often court-ordered in divorce actions involving children.

PARTY: A person involved in a court case, either as a petitioner or respondent.

PATERNITY (PARENTAGE) ACTION: A lawsuit used to determine whether a designated individual is the father of a specific child or children.

PETITIONER: The person who files the legal paper that begins a court case.

PLEADINGS: The legal documents filed in court, such as the Original Petition for Divorce and Original Answer.

POSTNUPTIAL (POSTMARITAL) AGREEMENT: A postnuptial agreement is an agreement between spouses made during marriage to govern division of assets and debt and to provide support in the event of divorce.

PRENUPTIAL (PREMARITAL) AGREEMENT: Also called a "prenup," this is an agreement between prospective spouses made in contemplation of marriage and to be effective on marriage. Premarital agreements allow persons about to marry to confirm and modify the characterization of property.

PRIMARY RESIDENCE: The home in which the children spend most of their time.

PROCESS SERVER: Person who serves legal papers on those being sued.

PRO SE LITIGANT: A person who appears in court without the assistance of a lawyer.

-Q-

QUALIFIED DOMESTIC RELATIONS ORDER: Called a Quadro, the most common use is for the division of retirement benefits on divorce. The QDRO is an order signed by the judge directed to a retirement plan administrator, which permits a non-employee former spouse to receive his or her share of retirement benefits directly.

-R-

RESPONDENT: The person who is served with a petition for divorce.

RETIREMENT BENEFITS – DEFINED BENEFIT PLAN: A defined benefit plan promises employees a monthly benefit beginning at retirement, and calculates the benefit factors specific to each plan, such as years of service, age and salary.

RETIREMENT BENEFITS – DEFINED CONTRI-BUTION PLAN: An employee participating in a defined contribution plan has an individual account to which generally both the employer and the employee make contributions.

-S-

SEPARATE PROPERTY: A spouse's separate property consists of property owned or claimed by the spouse before marriage; property acquired by a spouse during marriage by gift or inheritance; and recovery for personal injuries sustained by the spouse during marriage, except for any recovery for loss of earning capacity during marriage. A court cannot divest a spouse of his or her separate property in dividing the marital estate on divorce. A spouse claiming that disputed property is his or her separate property must prove that the property is separate property.

SERVICE: When a copy of a divorce petition (or other pleading) that has been filed by the court is delivered by a constable or private process server to the other party.

SETTLEMENT AGREEMENT: A document that sets out the agreement between the two parties when a divorce is settled.

STANDING ORDER: The purpose of a temporary injunction is to preserve the status quo during the pendency of the case. The injunction prohibits the spouses from doing or failing to do certain things, such as prohibiting the parties from spending funds in an amount in excess of reasonable and necessary living expenses, and preventing the dissipation, destruction or transfer of the parties' property during the pendency of the proceeding.

STOCK OPTION: The right to buy a designated stock at anytime within a specified period at a determinable price. Stock options may be vested or unvested.

SUBPOENA: A document served on a person, requiring an appearance at a certain time and place to testify and/or bring designated documents.

-T-

TEMPORARY ORDERS: Temporary orders entered during the divorce case can accomplish many things, including award the occupancy of the marital home to one of the parties, establish temporary custody and visitation of the parties' children, direct payment of temporary spousal or child support, direct a party to pay interim attorney's fees and direct the parties to provide an inventory and appraisement of their property.

TEMPORARY RESTRAINING ORDER: When a divorce suit has been filed, the court may, without notice to the other party, grant a temporary restraining order to preserve and protect the parties' property. Such an order may prohibit a party from spending money or withdrawing funds other than for reasonable and necessary living expenses, business expenses and attorney's fees. The temporary restraining order lasts for 14 days, unless an extension is granted, and is typically turned into a temporary injunction that is applicable to both parties.

TRIAL: The final hearing that decides all issues in a contested case.

-V-

VALUATION: The process by which the value of an asset is determined. The court may consider various types of evidence in determining the value of the parties' marital property.

VENUE: The jurisdiction where the case is heard.

APPENDIX C

Child Support Guidelines

Georgia lawmakers rewrote state laws governing child support in 2006, and the sweeping changes touched nearly every aspect of the issue. Possibly most importantly, the legislature created a system for establishing the base amount of child support.

The statutes are in the Official Code of Georgia Annotated. OCGA 19-6-50 through 19-6-53 deals with the Child Support Commission. OCGA 19-7-2 sets forth the parent's duty of support to the child.

To view the Georgia Schedule of Basic Child Support Obligations, which sets out payment guidelines, visit

http://www.legis.ga.gov/legis/2005_06/fulltext/sb382.htm

Here are a few of the critical points of Georgia's current child support laws:

- Georgia now considers the ability of both parents to pay in support of a child, a significant switch from older laws placing the responsibility primarily on the obligated parent. This reflects an increase in two-income families and of joint custody arrangements.
- The state provides new, markedly different guidelines, although judges and juries retain some discretion based on evidence presented during the divorce to deviate from the guidelines.
- Child support generally continues until a minor child reaches the age of majority, or 18 years old. Exceptions generally include the child's death, marriage or emancipation.
- The court may order support to continue for a child who has not completed secondary education by age 18, but that support ends at age 20.

- The formulae to calculate support begin with identifying the gross income of each parent, including salaries, commissions, bonuses and capital gains. The self-employed must calculate income against reasonable expenses of self-employment or business operations needed to produce income. Excessive promotional costs, travel, vehicle or personal living expenses are not considered reasonable and could count as income.

- Employment fringe benefits may count as income if they significantly reduce personal living expenses. An employer-provided company car, housing or room and board could each qualify as income.

- Some money is exempt. Child support payments received for the benefit of a child of another relationship do not count as income. Also, assistance programs such as food stamps or state aid programs don't figure into the calculation.

- A court weighs all of the variables to create a combined income calculation used as a basis for establishing child support.

- The judge or jury must adjust the parent's gross income based on pre-existing child support orders, self employment and Medicare taxes and other children living in the parent's household to whom the parent owes a duty of support.

- After calculation of the adjusted gross income of each parent, child support is based on the combined adjusted monthly income of the two parents. The matrix considers the combined adjusted income and the number of children in need of support.

- After determining the parent's child support obligation, the judge or jury shall consider the parent's work-related child care costs and health insurance premiums in the calculations to determine child support.

- The judge or jury may deviate from the presumptive amount of child support based on certain factors such as high or low income, travel expenses, mortgage costs, extraordinary medical and educational expense and extended parenting time with the noncustodial parent or when the child resides with both parents equally.

- Avoiding payment by taking a lower-paying job involves risk. The court can determine if a parent is voluntarily unemployed or underemployed and factor that into an award.
- Failing to pay child support can bring substantial penalties. The amount of a missed payment begins to accrue 7% interest per annum 30 days after the payment's due date.
- The person owed a child support payment faces no obligation to accept less money than the original payment plus the penalties, dissuading an ex from agreeing to pay the original amount if the penalty is forgiven.
- The court can reduce or waive the penalty based on an evaluation of considerations such as substantial hardship and the parent's past reliability for payment. The court, though, can also weigh a reduction against any possible harm to the parent owed the money.

APPENDIX D

Preparing For Your Deposition

I.   WHAT IS A DEPOSITION?

A deposition is a commonly used pretrial discovery device. You, as the deponent, are placed under oath and will answer questions asked by your spouse's attorney in front of a court reporter. The questions and answers will be recorded by the court reporter who will prepare a written transcript of the deposition. Your deposition may also be videotaped.

Your deposition must be taken seriously, as you will be testifying in your deposition just as if you were testifying in court. While rare, anyone falsifying a deposition could face perjury charges.

II.   PURPOSE OF A DEPOSITION

The main reasons for a deposition are as follows:

A. Your spouse's attorney wants to find out your knowledge regarding the issues in your divorce action. He or she is interested in what your story is now and what it is going to be at trial.

B. Your spouse's attorney wants to size up your demeanor and determine what type of witness you will make at trial.

C. Your spouse's attorney wants to nail down your version of the facts before trial so that they know in advance what your testimony will be at trial.

D. Your spouse's attorney wants to catch you in a lie or

an omission that can be used at trial to show that you are not honest and cast doubt on the veracity of your testimony. The transcript of your deposition may be used at trial by the opposing attorney to point out any trial testimony that varies from your deposition testimony.

Your spouse's attorney has every right to take your deposition. Your attorney also has the right to ask questions of you during the deposition, but most often your attorney will only ask questions to clarify an answer that may have been misleading or confusing.

Avoid the natural tendency to launch into your entire version of the case. This is not the proper time or place. Briefly and concisely answer only the question asked.

The testimony given in your deposition can be used in the trial of your case. A well-done deposition can have a positive effect on your case — the opposing attorney can see that you are an excellent witness and that you have a good case. Your chances of settlement will then be greatly improved.

III. WHO WILL BE PRESENT AT THE DEPOSITION

Depositions are usually taken in a conference room at the opposing attorney's office. The people typically in attendance are the parties, their attorneys and the court reporter. Spouses of the parties may also attend the deposition. Occasionally, a legal assistant will be present at the deposition. No judge is present.

IV. LENGTH OF DEPOSITION

The length of your deposition will depend on the complexity of the issues in your case, as well as the number of questions opposing counsel asks you. Do not make any other appointments or commitments on the day of your deposition. Georgia law limits a deposition to seven hours.

V.   QUESTIONS ASKED

Attorneys have the right to ask a number of questions. Some of the topics discussed at your deposition will not be admissible at trial. Unless your attorney instructs you not to answer a particular question, you must answer the question, even if your attorney objects to the question.

While opposing counsel may act like your friend in order to get you to relax and trust him or her, do not let your guard down. On the other hand, opposing counsel may try to wear you down by being confrontational, relentless and harassing. Regardless of the technique used, always be on guard and maintain a calm composure.

VI.   OBJECTIONS BY YOUR ATTORNEY

Your attorney will protect you from any improper questions by opposing counsel. Rarely will your attorney ask you any questions. The objections that can be made during the deposition are (1) leading, (2) form and (3) nonresponsive. Attorneys may also object and instruct the witness not to answer questions seeking privileged information. If the opposing attorney asks an improper question, your attorney may make an objection (e.g., "I object to the question on the ground of attorney-client privilege."). If your attorney ever instructs you not to answer a question, do not answer the question.

VII. HOW SHOULD I DRESS?

Your personal appearance should be conservative, neat, clean, and comfortable. Business or business/casual attire is appropriate. Your appearance should indicate that you are taking this matter and your deposition seriously. If your deposition will be videotaped, it is especially important for you to dress appropriately.

VIII.   THE COURT REPORTER'S ROLE

The court reporter is present to administer the oath (under which you swear to tell the truth) and record everything that you, the opposing attorney and your attorney say during the deposition. The court reporter is neutral and does not decide or mediate any disputes between the attorneys or parties. After the deposition, the court reporter prepares a written transcript of your deposition testimony and sends it to the attorneys.

IX. PREPARING FOR YOUR DEPOSITION

A. Review the Pleadings and Discovery Responses

In preparing for your deposition, review all of the pleadings filed in your case, as well as any affidavits, motions and discovery responses. Make sure that you understand the allegations, requests, causes of action and/or defenses raised in these documents.

B. Gather Any Requested Documents

You may have been requested to bring documents to your deposition. If the notice of your deposition includes a document request, you must gather documents, review them with your attorney and bring them to your deposition. If you have not been asked to bring documents to your deposition, do not bring anything. Leave your briefcase, calendar, PDA, etc., at home. You are not required to, and should not bring, any documents that you are not expressly requested to bring. Even if you think that a particular document is important, discuss the matter with your attorney before bringing it to your deposition.

Letters and e-mail between you and your attorney or his or her staff, and any memos or other documents prepared solely by your attorney or his staff, or prepared by you at the request of and for your attorney, are usually protected by law from being disclosed under the "attorney-client privilege" and the "work-product privilege." You should not produce such documents. If it appears to you that the request for documents would include documents that are privileged and confidential, bring this to the attention of your attorney.

If a document has not been requested, do not agree to supply documents or information. If you are asked to supply documents or information, refer the request to your counsel.

C. Conference with Your Attorney

Before the deposition, you and your attorney will have a conference to discuss the documents you are to bring to your deposition and what you can expect during your deposition. It is important that you be totally candid and tell the complete truth to your attorney, even if it appears to be damaging to your case.

It is okay to admit in your deposition that you have met and consulted with your attorney prior to your deposition. Anything that you and your attorney discuss is confidential and should not be revealed to the other side. If the opposing attorney asks you a question that your attorney believes you should not answer as it is an attorney-client communication, your attorney will object to the question and instruct you not to answer it.

Private conferences with your attorney are improper except to determine if a privilege should be asserted, although they may be held during agreed recesses and adjournments.

X.   ANSWERING QUESTIONS

A. Give Truthful and Accurate Testimony

In responding to the questions you are asked, you should always give truthful and accurate testimony. At the beginning of your deposition, you take an oath to tell the truth. You must tell the truth even if it is damaging to your case. If your testimony is not truthful and accurate, opposing counsel can later use your testimony against you at trial.

The following tips will help you give truthful and accurate testimony:

1.Your answers must be based upon your personal knowledge. Never volunteer your opinion unless expressly asked to do so. Never guess or speculate about a fact. If you did not personally witness or observe something, then you are justified in saying that you do not know the answer, even though you may have heard second-hand facts or information. Additionally, if you are asked why a certain decision was made but you did not participate in making the decision, you should say that you do not know why the decision was made. Similarly, do not speculate as to what "probably" happened. Your deposition testimony should rest upon first hand knowledge and a clear memory, not upon hearsay or speculation.

2. If you do not know the answer to a question, say so. If you cannot remember, say so.

3. If you are not sure of a particular fact, qualify your answer by beginning "to the best of my recollection."

4. Do not let opposing counsel put words in your mouth. If the opposing attorney attempts to summarize facts or testimony, listen very carefully to his or her summary and do not agree with it unless it is completely accurate. If it is not, simply state that you do not agree with the summary. If the introductory clause to a question contains any inaccurate information, be certain to specify the inaccurate information contained in the question prior to answering the question. If the question asked calls for a "yes" or "no" answer, and that type of answer does not accurately reflect the facts, you are not required to answer only "yes" or "no." Indicate that you are unable to do this.

5. Do not be intimidated by insinuations by the opposing attorney regarding your lack of truthfulness. If the attorney says, "You mean to tell me that you are willing to sit here under oath and swear to that fact?," remain calm, look the attorney in the eye and say, "I have just testified to that fact under oath."

6. Be careful of questions that ask "is that all?" It is okay to say "to the best of my knowledge at this time."

7. You may be asked a question like: "Tell me all of the negative qualities of your spouse as a parent." The lawyer asking the question is trying to put you in a box and limit you at trial to what your answer was in your deposition. If you are asked this type of question, give as many reasons as you can, but when you finish, give yourself an escape route out of the box by saying, "I am sure there are other reasons, but I cannot think of them right now."Another way an attorney will try to put a box around your testimony is to ask you to tell everything you can remember about a certain event. Always leave yourself an exit route out of the box by saying, "That is all I can remember at this time."

8. Be careful about events that happened a long time ago. For example, if you are asked about some event that occurred many years ago, and you do not remember the exact time or date, simply say so. Do not guess.

9. You can phrase your answers at times in a manner that may be helpful to your case. For example, instead of simply saying "yes," a more heart-felt response might be "of course" or "absolutely."

10. Avoid using "always" and "never."

11. If opposing counsel asks you about certain documents, you may ask to see the document before you answer the questions. When confronted with documents, examine them carefully. If you haven't seen a particular document before or did not prepare it, don't try to guess what it means. Do not vouch for the accuracy of someone else's document.

12. If at any time during the deposition you realize you have given an erroneous answer, correct your answer as soon as you recognize your error.

13. Watch out for compound questions.

14. If your testimony is based upon an approximation, you should make this clear to the examining lawyer. Any testimony that is based on estimates should be given only where the record unequivocally reflects that this is the basis for the testimony.

15. Do not guess details. Be careful of giving exact information (such as measurements, dates, time intervals and business statistics) if you are uncertain about the details, particularly when the information is available in some business or other records. If you are asked a question of this nature and you are uncertain, respond that you do not remember the exact information. If the information requested is available from certain records, you may add that any answer you give will be your best estimate only, and is subject to verification through applicable records.

B. Listen to the Question and Make Sure you Understand It.

Listen to the question carefully and make sure you understand it before you answer. Pause for a few seconds before responding to each question to make sure that you understand the question and think about the answer. If you did not hear or understand the question, politely inform the opposing counsel to repeat or explain the question.

C. Do Not Volunteer Information

Answer the question you are asked as concisely as possible and then stop. Give as short an answer as possible, and be sure your response is narrowed to the exact question asked. There is usually no benefit to volunteering information. Your deposition is not the time to tell your side of the story. Following are some tips for answering questions without volunteering information:

1. Do not give your opinion regarding any fact or issue unless you are asked for your opinion—just answer the question that you are asked.

2. If the opposing counsel asks you a question that calls for a "yes" or "no" answer, simply answer "yes" or "no."

3. Avoid rambling answers—do not explain details unless you are requested to do so.

4. Even if the opposing attorney pauses as though he or she is waiting for you to give an explanation, stop talking and wait for the next question.

5. Do not try to anticipate the answer to the next question that you will be asked.

6. Do not voluntarily offer information to the opposing attorney as to where he or she can find information being inquired about unless expressly asked to do so.

7. Do not refer to or volunteer to provide any documents unless expressly requested to do so.

8. Do not let opposing counsel interrupt your full answer. If this happens, politely state that you were not through with your answer and ask if you may finish it.

XI. THINGS TO AVOID

A. Avoid Becoming Nervous or Flustered.

Remember that the opposing attorney is sizing up your demeanor as a witness during your deposition (which may greatly affect settlement negotiations). Therefore, your conduct, appearance and demeanor at your deposition is important. It is important to present a good impression. You should try to relax, remain calm and not appear nervous. Speak loudly and positively and with self assurance. There is no need to show fear or anxiety or be afraid to answer truthfully.

B. Avoid Getting Angry or Mad.

It is important that you conduct yourself in a reasonable and mature fashion during your deposition. Avoid losing your temper, getting mad or upset, cursing or engaging in name calling. Opposing counsel may try to provoke you so that you hurt your case—do not let this happen. Your conduct should be polite, courteous and calm. Do not interrupt opposing counsel's questions. Never argue with opposing counsel.

279

C. Avoid Humor.

Avoid all jokes or wisecracks in a deposition. What may at the time seem like an innocent joke may not appear to be a joking matter in the written transcript. Never try to get the upper hand on the opposing attorney by using some clever comeback or by turning the tables and asking him or her questions.

D. Avoid Referring to Documents.

Never refer to any document to refresh your memory unless you have been authorized to do so by your attorney. A rule of law in Georgia is that if a deponent is asked a question, and he or she stops and looks at a document in order to refresh his memory, then that document is required to be disclosed and handed over to the opposing attorney.

XII. READING AND SIGNING THE DEPOSITION

After your deposition is concluded, the court reporter will transcribe the record into a typed written deposition transcript. You will then be given an opportunity to read the deposition and make corrections, either in misspellings, mistaken dates or other such changes. You will also need to give a reason for each such change.

APPENDIX E

Post-Divorce Checklist

Checklist	Needs to be Done	Completed
Prepare Deeds and File		
Real Property Deeds		
Estate Documents		
Will		
Medical Directive		
Power of Attorney		
Name Change (Probate Court)		
Automobile Titles		
Automobile Insurance		
Insurance Forms		
Life Insurance Provisions - Notify Carrier of Beneficiary Change		
Health Insurance Provisions - Notify carrier and order new identification card(s)		
Bank Accounts		
Safety Deposit Box		
Tax-IRS Forms		
IRS Form 8332 (Dependency Exemption)		
Form W-4		
Retirement Accounts / IRA / Pension		
QDRO		
Income Withholding Orders		

APPENDIX F

IRS Form 8332

Dependent Exemption

Form **8332**	**Release of Claim to Exemption**	OMB No. 1545-0915
(Rev. December 2000)	**for Child of Divorced or Separated Parents**	
Department of the Treasury Internal Revenue Service	▶ **Attach** to noncustodial parent's return **each year** exemption is claimed. Caution: *Do not use this form if you were never married.*	Attachment Sequence No. **115**

Name of noncustodial parent claiming exemption	Noncustodial parent's social security number (SSN) ▶	⋮ ⋮

Part I	**Release of Claim to Exemption for Current Year**

I agree not to claim an exemption for_____
Name(s) of child (or children)

for the tax year 20_____ .

_____	⋮ ⋮	
Signature of custodial parent releasing claim to exemption	Custodial parent's SSN	Date

Note: *If you choose not to claim an exemption for this child (or children) for future tax years, also complete Part II.*

Part II	**Release of Claim to Exemption for Future Years** (If completed, see **Noncustodial parent** below.)

I agree not to claim an exemption for_____
Name(s) of child (or children)

for the tax year(s)_____ .
(Specify. See instructions.)

_____	⋮ ⋮	
Signature of custodial parent releasing claim to exemption	Custodial parent's SSN	Date

General Instructions

Purpose of form. If you are a **custodial parent** and you were ever married to the child's **noncustodial parent**, you may use this form to release your claim to your child's exemption. To do so, complete this form (or a similar statement containing the same information required by this form) and give it to the noncustodial parent who will claim the child's exemption. The noncustodial parent must attach this form or similar statement to his or her tax return **each year** the exemption is claimed.

You are the **custodial parent** if you had custody of the child for most of the year. You are the **noncustodial parent** if you had custody for a shorter period of time or did not have custody at all. For the definition of custody, see **Pub. 501,** Exemptions, Standard Deduction, and Filing Information.

Support test for children of divorced or separated parents. Generally, the custodial parent is treated as having provided over half of the child's support if:

• The child received over half of his or her total support for the year from one or both of the parents **and**

• The child was in the custody of one or both of the parents for more than half of the year.

Note: *Public assistance payments, such as Temporary Assistance for Needy Families (TANF), are not support provided by the parents.*

For this support test to apply, the parents must be one of the following:

• Divorced or legally separated under a decree of divorce or separate maintenance,

• Separated under a written separation agreement, **or**

• Living apart at all times during the last 6 months of the year.

Caution: *This support test does not apply to parents who never married each other.*

If the support test applies, and the other four dependency tests in your tax return

instruction booklet are also met, the custodial parent can claim the child's exemption.

Exception. The custodial parent will not be treated as having provided over half of the child's support if **any** of the following apply.

• The custodial parent agrees not to claim the child's exemption by signing this form or similar statement.

• The child is treated as having received over half of his or her total support from a person under a multiple support agreement (**Form 2120,** Multiple Support Declaration).

• A pre-1985 divorce decree or written separation agreement states that the noncustodial parent can claim the child as a dependent. But the custodial parent must provide at least $600 for the child's support during the year. This rule does not apply if the decree or agreement was changed after 1984 to say that the noncustodial parent cannot claim the child as a dependent.

Additional information. For more details, see **Pub. 504,** Divorced or Separated Individuals.

Specific Instructions

Custodial parent. You may agree to release your claim to the child's exemption for the current tax year or for future years, or both.

• Complete **Part I** if you agree to release your claim to the child's exemption for the current tax year.

• Complete **Part II** if you agree to release your claim to the child's exemption for any or all future years. If you do, write the specific future year(s) or "all future years" in the space provided in Part II.

TIP To help ensure future support, you may not want to release your claim to the child's exemption for future years.

Noncustodial parent. Attach this form or similar statement to your tax return for **each year** you claim the child's exemption. You may claim the exemption **only** if the other four dependency tests in your tax return instruction booklet are met.

Note: *If the custodial parent released his or her claim to the child's exemption for any future year, you **must** attach a copy of this form or similar statement to your tax return for each future year that you claim the exemption. **Keep a copy for your records.***

Paperwork Reduction Act Notice. We ask for the information on this form to carry out the Internal Revenue laws of the United States. You are required to give us the information. We need it to ensure that you are complying with these laws and to allow us to figure and collect the right amount of tax.

You are not required to provide the information requested on a form that is subject to the Paperwork Reduction Act unless the form displays a valid OMB control number. Books or records relating to a form or its instructions must be retained as long as their contents may become material in the administration of any Internal Revenue law. Generally, tax returns and return information are confidential, as required by Internal Revenue Code section 6103.

The time needed to complete and file this form will vary depending on individual circumstances. The estimated average time is:

Recordkeeping	7 min.
Learning about the law or the form	5 min.
Preparing the form	7 min.
Copying, assembling, and sending the form to the IRS	. . 14 min.

If you have comments concerning the accuracy of these time estimates or suggestions for making this form simpler, we would be happy to hear from you. You can write to the Tax Forms Committee, Western Area Distribution Center, Rancho Cordova, CA 95743-0001. **Do not** send the form to this address. Instead, see the Instructions for Form 1040 or Form 1040A.

Cat. No. 13910F

Form **8332** (Rev. 12-2000)

APPENDIX G

Credit Report Request Letter

Credit Report Request Letter

The address of local and national credit bureau reporting firms is found in the Yellow Pages.

Name
Address
City, State, Zip

Date

Credit Bureau
Address
City, State Zip

Re: [First] [Middle Initial] [Maiden] [Last]
      SSN

This is to request that a copy of my entire credit history/report be mailed to me at the above address. I have enclosed a check in the amount of $_____ to cover the cost of the report and shipping.

Thank you in advance for your prompt response to my request.

Very truly yours,

[Name]

Appendix 12.
Estimated Monthly Living Expenses

APPENDIX H

Social Security Request Letter

Request for Earnings and Benefit Estimate Statement

☐ Please check this box if you want to get your statement in Spanish instead of English.

Please print or type your answers. When you have completed the form, fold it and mail it to us. (If you prefer to send your request using the Internet, contact us at http://www.ssa.gov)

1. Name shown on your Social Security card:

First Name   Middle Initial

Last Name Only

2. Your Social Security number as shown on your card:

☐☐☐-☐☐-☐☐☐☐

3. Your date of birth (Mo.-Day-Yr.):

☐☐-☐☐-☐☐

4. Other Social Security numbers you have used:

☐☐☐-☐☐-☐☐☐☐
☐☐☐-☐☐-☐☐☐☐

5. Your sex: ☐ Male ☐ Female

Form SSA-7004-SM Internet (6-98) Destroy prior editions

For items 6 and 8 show only earnings covered by Social Security. Do NOT include wages from State, local or Federal Government employment that are NOT covered for Social Security or that are covered ONLY by Medicare.

6. Show your actual earnings (wages and/or net self-employment income) for last year and your estimated earnings for this year.

A. Last year's actual earnings: (Dollars Only)

$ ☐☐☐,☐☐☐.0 0

B. This year's estimated earnings: (Dollars Only)

$ ☐☐☐,☐☐☐.0 0

7. Show the age at which you plan to stop working.

☐☐ (Show only one age)

8. Below, show the average yearly amount (not your total future lifetime earnings) that you think you will earn between now and when you plan to stop working. Include performance or scheduled pay increases or bonuses, but not cost-of-living increases.

If you expect to earn significantly more or less in the future due to promotions, job changes, part-time work, or an absence from the work force, enter the amount that most closely reflects your future average yearly earnings.

If you don't expect any significant changes, show the same amount you are earning now (the amount in 6B).

Future average yearly earnings: (Dollars Only)

$ ☐☐☐,☐☐☐.0 0

9. Do you want us to send the statement:
- To you? Enter your name and mailing address.
- To someone else (your accountant, pension plan, etc.)? Enter your name with "c/o" and the name and address of that person or organization.

Name

Street Address (Include Apt. No., P.O. Box, or Rural Route)

City   State   Zip Code

Notice:
I am asking for information about my own Social Security record or the record of a person I am authorized to represent. I understand that if I deliberately request information under false pretenses, I may be guilty of a Federal crime and could be fined and/or imprisoned. I authorize you to use a contractor to send the statement of earnings and benefit estimates to the person named in item 9.

▲

Please sign your name (Do Not Print)

Date   (Area Code) Daytime Telephone No.

Form Approved
OMB No. 0960-0466   SP

Request for Earnings and Benefit Estimate Statement

Thank you for requesting this statement.

After you complete and return this form, we will--within 4 to 6 weeks--send you:

- a record of your earnings history and an estimate of how much you have paid in Social Security taxes, and
- estimates of benefits you (and your family) may be eligible for now and in the future.

We're pleased to furnish you with this information and we hope you'll find it useful in planning your financial future.

Social Security is more than just a program for retired people. It helps people of all ages in many ways. Whether you're young or old, male or female, single or with a family--Social Security can help you when you need it most. It can help support your family in the event of your death and pay you benefits if you become severly disabled.

If you have questions about Social Security or this form, please call our toll-free number, 1-800-772-1213.

Kenneth S. Apfel

Kenneth S. Apfel
Commissioner of Social Security

Mailing Address

Social Security Administration
Wilkes Barre Data Operations Center
PO Box 7004
Wilkes Barre PA 18767-7004

About The Privacy Act

Social Security is allowed to collect the facts on this form under Section 205 of the Social Security Act. We need them to quickly identify your record and prepare the earnings statement you asked us for. Giving us these facts is voluntary. However, without them we may not be able to give you an earnings and benefit estimate statement. Neither the Social Security Administration nor its contractor will use the information for any other purpose.

Paperwork Reduction Act Notice and Time It Takes Statement

The Paperwork Reduction Act of 1995 requires us to notify you that this information collection is in accordance with the clearance requirements of section 3507 of the Paperwork Reduction Act of 1995. We may not conduct or sponsor, and you are not required to respond to, a collection of information unless it displays a valid OMB control number. We estimate that it will take you about 5 minutes to complete this form. This includes the time it will take to read the instructions, gather the necessary facts and fill out the form.

APPENDIX I

Recommended books on the financial and emotional sides of divorce, with no specific references to Georgia:

What Every Woman Should Know About Divorce and Custody by Gayle Rosenwald Smith and Sally Abrahms

Divorce Rules for Men: A Man to Man Guide for Managing Your Split and Saving Thousands by Martin M. Shenkman and Michael J. Hamilton

Divorce and Money: Everything You Need to Know by Gayle Rosenwald Smith

Getting Divorced Without Ruining Your Life by Sam Margulies

Financial Custody: You, Your Money and Divorce by Joan Coullahan and Sue van der Linden

How to Fall Out of Love: How to Free Yourself of Love That Hurts — and Find the Love that Heals by Robert Judd and Dr. Debora Phillips

Uncoupling: Turning Points in Intimate Relationships by Diane Vaughan

Coming Apart: Why Relationships End and How to Live Through the Ending of Yours by Daphne Rose Kingma

The Seven Principles for Making Marriage Work by John
M. Gottman

Getting the Love You Want: A Guide for Couples by
Harville Hendrix

*The Five Love Languages: How to Express Heartfelt
Commitment to Your Mate* by Gary Chapman

*Passionate Marriage: Love, Sex, and Intimacy in
Emotionally Committed Relationship* by David Schnarch

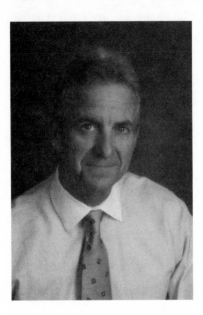

"Everyone needs the information in this book, even if you intend to stay married the rest of your life," says John C. Mayoue. "If your spouse dies, is incapacitated or simply abandons the family, these same rules apply."

Mayoue, one of the South's most renowned family law attorneys, is a prolific writer on family topics, has appeared many times on CNN, and has been widely quoted in magazines and newspapers across the country. His clients include Marianne Gingrich, ex-wife of former U.S. House Speaker Newt Gingrich; Jane Fonda, former wife of billionaire Ted Turner; and David Justice, a former professional baseball player Mayoue represented in a divorce from actress Halle Berry.

Mayoue is contributing his royalties from the sale of this book to Camp Sunshine, an Atlanta-based facility devoted to children with cancer and their families.

Mayoue contributes time and money to many worthwhile causes. In addition, he is available to speak to groups on the financial aspects of divorce and other child and family-related topics. He can be reached at the law firm of Warner, Mayoue, Bates & Nolen, P.C., 3350 Riverwood Pkwy, Suite 2300, Atlanta, GA 30339; 770 951-2700 voice, 770 951-2200 facsimile; Email: jmayoue@wmbnlaw.com.